Comments to Lou are welcome. He can be reached at:
LPanesi@bellsouth.net

READER REVIEWS

Hard to Put Down
"The author's ability to recall conversations makes the book captivating and you want to keep reading it."

Courage
"Louis Panesi shows great courage to write this about the abuse and his passion to overcome these circumstances in his life."

Important Story, Well Written
"I read this book in one day. It was well-written. Poignant. Heartwrenching."

Best Book of the Year
"This book is, first of all, a phenomenal read. It's well-written, interesting and answers many questions about the human condition."

Easy to Read and Identify With Author
"What gets me is that this particular mental torture the father pressed onto his son was nothing short of CRIMINAL. This story underlines the quote "Any one can be a father, but it takes someone special to be a Daddy.""

A Pilot's Battle Between the Heavens and Hell of his Youth
"This was one of those books I couldn't put down and fortunately I didn't have to. Even though the story ends, you will be inspired with the feeling Mr. Panesi's life, although matured, has just begun."

"For a period of several years Panesi visited Dr. Shoemaker and his recounting of his sessions with the good doctor is a fascinating read. In fact, without having any formal training as a writer, Panesi understands more of the importance of economy of language and maintaining a good pace than many an experienced author."

~ Norm Goldman, "Top 500 Reviewer" Amazon.com, Editor & Publisher of Bookpleasures

121
University
Place

The True Story of a Homeless,

Tortured Boy and the Psychiatrist

Who Saved His Life

Louis Panesi

121 University Place

Louis Panesi

S E C O N D   E D I T I O N

ISBN: 978-0-9792166-0-2

Pass It on Publishing

PINEVILLE, NC

Requests for permission or further information should be addressed to:
Pass it on Publishing, 12512 Diamond Drive, Pineville, NC 28134

Printed in the United States of America

This book is dedicated to
Robert J. Shoemaker, M.D.

Thank you Dr. Shoemaker. I wrote this book for you.
I love you.
I miss you. I'll never forget you.

Acknowledgments

Many thanks to those who supported me in
writing and designing this book:
Barbara McNichol, editor
Caron B. Goode, Ed.D., coach and mentor
Nancy Cleary, designer and publishing consultant
Shawn Dobbins, illustrator
Kim Honeycutt for her encouragement
Marca Storey, therapist
Jill Eilenberger, therapist
Beth Barrineau Ward, therapist
Kim Honeycutt, therapist
James E. Lee, M.D., neuropsychiatrist
Nancy Richter, proof-reader and friend
Diane Trachtenberg, coach and mentor
Frank Palombi
Elizabeth Bennett Holmes
Chuck Steinmiller
Lester J. Bolanovich, Psychiatrist
Roberto Clemente, my childhood hero

A special heartfelt thank you to my dermatologist, William S. Gibson,
M.D., who introduced me to Dr. Shoemaker
and changed my life forever.

Table of Contents

Warning

This is a true story and features subject matter that some readers may find disturbing. Because it contains strong language spoken in therapy sessions, reader discretion is advised.

CHAPTER 1
A Bloody Back Leads To My Lucky Break

"People, even more than things, have to be restored, renewed, revived, reclaimed, and redeemed; never throw out anyone."

- Audrey Hepburn

May 1975

I'm startled by a car horn honking behind me. I'm stopped at a red light in Oakland where the University of Pittsburgh is located. I must have been daydreaming. I'm nervous and scared because I'm on my way to my dermatologist's office. I know I'll have to take off my shirt in front of people again. I hate doing that. I know they're professionals, but it still bothers me. Why shouldn't it? Even *I* feel frightened every time I see my back in the mirror.

Why does it bleed all the time? I can't even sit back on my seat without it hurting. This has been going on since the tenth grade. Blood keeps oozing through my shirt and it won't stop. I wear extra undershirts to soak it up. Now I have to wear three of them under my regular shirt. I'm tired of wearing all these shirts. It's hot. It's going to be 80 degrees today. I don't want to wear all of these shirts.

As I drive down Fifth Avenue toward the doctor's office, I see all these beautiful girls walking to class. Tears well up in my eyes. I know deep down I'll never be able to talk to girls like them. I'm only three months away from being a 20-year-old virgin.

Who would want *me*, after all? My own family hates me and has disowned me. Last Saturday, my dad and grandpap threw me out of the house. They'd always told me I was hopeless. They said I'd never amount to anything, that I'm a loser.

I guess they're right. My car is falling apart. I'm working as a janitor at the Holiday Inn in Greentree. At least the homeless shelter took me in. The people there are nice to me.

I wish Dr. Gibson would see me by himself. Why does he have to have two nurses with him? The fact that they're young and pretty makes it even worse. I'm sure they cringe when they see me on the exam table. Why can't he help me? He's my fourth dermatologist in the last four years. So far, no one has been able to cure my bloody back.

I walk into his office on the 5th floor of the Medical Arts building. His office manager, Gloria, greets me with a smile. She's about 50 and really nice. She's always friendly to me. Everyone who works for Dr. Gibson is nice. Every time I come here, they always seem to be having fun at work. Gloria says . . .

Lou, Dr. Gibson will be with you in a minute.

OK.

I take a seat in the waiting room with the other people. I make sure not to make eye contact with anyone. I pick up a magazine and pretend to read. Right away I start biting my fingernails, or what's left of them. I bite them to the point that they bleed. After a few minutes, Dr. Gibson looks in and sees me. He smiles.

Hey, Lou, come on back. How are you?

Hi, Dr. Gibson. I'm OK.

Dr. Gibson is 58 years old, about 6' 1" and 190 pounds. He has slicked-back grayish hair. I think he's a great guy. Every time I come here, I see him laughing and kidding around with his staff and the other patients. I always force a smile when he greets me, but I usually don't interact much with him. I wish I could. I want him to know I like him.

Lou, you can go in the exam room on the right. I'll be with you in a few minutes.

OK.

I know the drill. I go in and take off my bloody shirts, then lie down on the exam table. I lie face down on my stomach and wait for him and his beautiful nurses to come in. This is the worst part. Minutes feel like hours. I close my eyes and feel like I'm waiting for the executioner to show up. Sometimes I wish that were true. At least I'd be put out of my misery.

Dr. Gibson finally walks in. I can tell he's smiling down at me as he says hello again. I don't look up. I keep my eyes closed and barely acknowledge him. I just want this to be over. I don't want to even see the nurses. Maybe I can leave today without having to look at them.

Dr. Gibson makes small talk with me, then begins his routine of using dry ice on my bloody back. Tears well up in my eyes, not only from pain but from the shame I feel. I keep my head down so no one can see me cry.

His treatment only lasts about 10 minutes. When he's finished, he usually wishes me well and tells me to make another appointment with Gloria two weeks away. This time is different.

Lou, after you get dressed, can you come back to my office? I'd like to see you for a minute.

What's this about? Maybe I'm in trouble. What did I do? I pay my bill every visit. What could he want? I get dressed and walk down the short hall to his office door. As I approach the door, I see him sitting at his desk looking at some papers.

Hey, Lou. Come in and close the door.

Yes, sir.

Have a seat.

I sit down. I see him looking right at me with a compassionate face.

Lou, I feel badly that I haven't been getting results with your back.

I nod.

I usually see good results with others from these treatments.

I nod again, trying to make eye contact with him. I hear his gentle voice and feel a little less afraid.

Lou, would you mind if I asked you a personal question?

No.

How is your home life?

What? Why does he care about that? *No one* cares. Suddenly something inside me bursts. I start crying and say . . .

It's terrible. I was kicked out of my house on Saturday.

Why?

Because I was sleeping at eight-thirty in the morning.

Where are you living now?

At Light of Life Ministries homeless shelter near Allegheny General Hospital.

As I say those words, I cry even harder. I don't know what's happening but I can't stop crying.

Why would they kick you out of the house?

I look down and shrug my shoulders. I manage to blurt out . . .

My dad hates my guts.

I'm now crying so hard, I can barely get the words out. Dr. Gibson hands me a box of Kleenex.

Lou, would you mind if I give you the number of a doctor friend of mine?

I keep my head down.

No, I wouldn't mind.

He is a psychiatrist. Would that bother you to see him?

No.

Lou, this man is my friend and a great doctor. I think he could help you more than I can.

I nod OK. Tears running down my cheeks, I glance up at Dr. Gibson with a look of thanks and gratitude.

Lou, here's his name and address. He's only one block from here. I'll call him for you. You'll like him. Lou, *he gets results.*

Dr. Gibson stands up and hands me the paper with this doctor's name. I put it in my pocket and stand up. Dr. Gibson walks me to the door. I take the elevator to the parking garage. When I get in my car, I take out the paper he gave me and read it. It says . . .

DR. ROBERT J. SHOEMAKER, M.D.
121 UNIVERSITY PLACE

CHAPTER 2
My First Visit With Dr. Shoemaker

"The gift we can offer is so simple a thing as hope."

- Daniel Berrigan

As I drive back to my homeless shelter, all I could think about was my upcoming visit with a *real* psychiatrist. I'd never even met a psychiatrist.

This is kind of weird because I just read a book by a psychiatrist two weeks before. The book was called *Compassion and Self Hate: An Alternative to Despair* by Theodore Isaac Rubin, MD. I found it at my cousin Ada Jean's house when she'd invited me over to dinner. After we ate, I looked at the books in her study—about ten book-shelves filled with great books. I don't know why, but I picked out Dr. Rubin's book and asked her if I could take it home with me.

From the first page, this book blew me away. I couldn't stop reading it. I finished it in two days. It was about 250 pages of a psychiatrist writing about what he learned from his patients during his 30 years of practice.

Dr. Rubin relayed stories about his patients and how their problems started in their childhood. He gave detailed accounts of their child-hoods and how it affected them as adults.

One story really blew my mind. It was about a female patient named Rosiland. She had skin coming off her arms and back, just like me. He explained that it stemmed from her dad making her feel guilty about sex when she was little. When Rosiland grew up and started having sex, this guilt really took over. Her skin became a mess. She went to dermatologist after dermatologist and none of them could help her, just like me! The doctor found out the root cause of her problem. Mostly, he talked her through it until she got better. She was *just like me*!

Wow. I want to meet one of these doctors.

I read the whole book again. And now I'm going to meet one of these talking doctors. I'm actually going to spend 45 minutes with one of these smart doctors. What a coincidence! Maybe this guy can do for me what Dr. Rubin did for Rosiland.

The next morning, I drive to my grandma's house in Carnegie. I wait until 10 o'clock because I knew my dad wouldn't be there at that time. Every time he sees me, he screams and yells and my grandma can't take it. I bring her my bloody undershirts and she puts them in the washing machine for me. She also makes me a sandwich and I put it in a bag so I have something to eat after I leave.

> Grandma, Dr. Gibson wants me to go see another doctor about my back.

> Why?

> He thinks this other doctor can help me more than he can.

She talks to me in her broken English.

> When you go see him?

> Tomorrow.

> You have money?

> No.

How much he charge?

I'm not sure.

Here, I give you $100. You bring back change, OK?

Yes. Thank you, Grandma.

I give her a kiss on the cheek.

She makes sure that her husband, my grandpap, doesn't see this. If he did, he would blow up and then tell my dad and they would make her life even more miserable than it already is.

Here, Louie, take these clean clothes with you.

OK. Thank you.

You eat OK?

Yes, Grandma. They feed us at eight o'clock in the morning and five in the afternoon. They are nice to me there.

As I head out the door, my grandma follows me and gives me one more hug before I drive away.

***

I find the psychiatrist's office. It's only one block away from The Cathedral of Learning on the University of Pittsburgh campus. I park my car in the parking lot adjacent to the six-story building and the attendant stamps my ticket. I take the elevator to the fourth floor and sit in the waiting room. My appointment is for 5 o'clock and I'm 20 minutes early. I don't want to be late. I see a waiting room with about six chairs in it. No one is sitting in there except me. I notice a sign on the wall that says "Robert J. Shoemaker, M.D." and another that says "C. Paul Scott, M.D."

I know I'm in the right place.

At 5 o'clock, I see Dr. Shoemaker's door open and a businessman who is about 50 years old leaves. I guess that was his last patient. That means I'm next. I am so filled with emotion. One part of me is scared; the other part is excited like a kid. If this doctor is anything like Dr. Rubin, I *know* he can help me with my back.

After a few minutes, the doctor's door opens again and a man walks up to me with a big smile on his face. He extends his hand to shake mine. I'm still sitting down.

> Hi, you must be Lou.

I meekly put out my hand.

> Yes, sir.

> Come in, Lou.

> OK.

> Boy, it's really getting hot outside.

> Yes. The radio said it's 87 degrees.

> Have a seat, Lou.

He points to a wooden chair in front of his desk.

I notice right away that he's friendly and easy to be around. He doesn't act the way I pictured a psychiatrist would act. He's too nice. I notice I am taller than he is. I'm 6'1" and I'd say he was about 5' 10". He looks like he's about Dr. Gibson's age—maybe 60—and a little heavy set—about 200 pounds. He has brown hair combed back and wears a suit and tie, not his doctor's coat.

I sit in the chair in front of his desk and he takes the seat behind it. His is a big swivel black leather chair that looks comfortable. His office isn't big but it seems cozy.

As I take my seat, I'm taking in his whole office with my eyes. Right away, I notice a couch to my left against the wall and a big chair next to it. That must be the psychoanalytic couch I read about. One end of the couch has a slight rise to it. This must be where patients put their heads, I think. The big chair is placed next to where a patient's head would rest. From what I had read, the psychiatrist sits at an angle so the patient on the couch can't see him. That positioning is supposed to be important.

> Dr. Gibson called me about you, Lou. He really thinks highly of you.

> He does?

> Yes.

> He is one of the nicest guys I've ever met.

> Bill is a great guy. I've known him for years.

I notice the doctor smiling and I feel comfortable. He looks a bit like Babe Ruth with his friendly, round face.

> Dr. Gibson thinks you might be able to help me with my back.

I stand and turn, lifting my shirt to show him all of the blood on it.

> Do you think you can help me?

> I can't promise you anything, Lou.

Have you ever seen anyone with this kind of problem?

Yes.

That answer made me feel good. At least he has a background in this type of problem. I notice him take out a cigarette and light it up. He then extends the pack to me.

Would you like a cigarette, Lou?

What? This guy is talking to me like I could be his friend or something. I can see he is smiling and being gentle with me.

No, thank you. I don't smoke.

You've never smoked?

No.

That's good. It's a bad habit. How old are you, Lou?

Nineteen. I'll be twenty on August fourth.

Oh, to be nineteen again.

I hate this age.

Why?

Because I'm always in trouble.

In what way?

My dad yells and screams at me every day. Well, not right now because I'm living at a homeless shelter.

What? You're living at a homeless shelter?

Yes.

How long have you been living there?

A week.

Why are you staying there?

Because my dad kicked me out of the house on Saturday.

Why?

Because I was sleeping in on my day off. It was eight-thirty in the morning and he barged into my room and took my clothes and threw them in the yard.

He threw your clothes in the yard?

Yeah.

Why did he do that?

I shrug my shoulders.

He hates me.

Were you out drinking?

No. I don't drink.

Drugs?

No. I've never taken any drugs.

Why do you think he hates you?

My dad and grandfather hate the fact that I am part Irish. They are full-blooded Italian and they hate Irish people.

Where is your mom?

In California. They are divorced. My dad lives with his mom and dad in Carnegie. That is where I was living until he kicked me out.

I can see that the doctor's face is pained as I tell him this. This makes me feel good. At least he can see that my family is weird. That's a relief.

I forgot to ask you how much to pay you.

I charge seventy-five dollars for a forty-five-minute session.

OK.

I put $75 on his desk.

He pushes it aside and thanks me.

Lou, would you like some tea?

No, thank you.

He pours some hot water into a cup with a tea bag in it.

Are you working, Lou?

Yes. I work in the housekeeping department at the Holiday Inn in Greentree. I used to work at the Marriott right next door but I quit that job.

Why did you quit?

Because on payday, we had to go into the supervisor's office to pick up our paychecks. I was too embarrassed to go in by myself, so I quit after two weeks.

So, Lou, tell me—how are you able to pay for this?

My grandma is paying for this. Now I'm at the Holiday Inn but I'm only part time so I don't get benefits. She feels bad for me. She knows that my dad and grandpap mistreat me. Also, she is the one who washes my undershirts and she sees how bloody they are. She worries about me.

Before I know it, my 45 minutes are up. Time goes so fast. I guess I'm talking nonstop. I don't want to leave. I have so much I want to tell him.

Lou, can you come back next week at the same time?

Yeah.

OK. I'll see you next Friday at five o'clock.

He writes it down on a card for me, hands me the card, and walks me to the door. He shakes my hand. I notice that he doesn't crush it like everyone else does.

Thank you, Dr. Shoemaker. Thank you very much. Do you think you can help me?

All I can tell you, Lou, is that I'll try my best.

OK.

As we part company at his door, tears fill my eyes. What a nice man he is. Just as nice as Dr. Gibson. It feels so good to have someone take an interest in me—someone who actually listens to me and lets me talk.

See you next week, Lou.

Bye.

As I drive back to the homeless shelter, a wave of hope goes through me. This guy was awesome. *He listened to me. He made me feel comfortable.*

I arrive at the shelter and lie on my bed to start reading my book again. I want to know more about psychiatry. I'm excited. I think this doctor can help me! I fall asleep reading and sleep soundly all the way through the night—the first time I had been able to do that in years.

CHAPTER 3
"It's All Bullshit"

"Difficulties are meant to rouse, not discourage.
The human spirit is to grow strong by conflict."
- William Ellery Channing

Before my second visit with Dr. Shoemaker, I'm able to find a place to stay. An older couple that lives only four houses down from my dad's is helping me out. Their names are Reba and Harold Siebert and they're actually like grandparents to me. They not only helped raise me, they also raised my mom. My mom lived with them from the age of 10 until she married my dad when she was 21. So, not only did they know me and my mom, they also knew the Panesi family as well as anyone. They know that my dad and grandfather treat me like crap. In fact, they would always try and stick up for me when they talked to them. It never did any good.

Here's my granpap talking to Harold in his broken English:

"Harold, that kid never going amount to anything as long as he has a hole in his ass."

"Luigi, quit talking like that. He's a good kid."

"He's a lazy bum. We always know he never amount to anything."

Reba and Harold own a duplex. Their tenant is a divorced man named Walt Kightlinger, who is about 55 years old. He owns the gas station at the end of our street. Everyone in the neighborhood knows him. When Reba and Harold told him that I was living at a homeless shelter on the north side, he told them I could rent out his second bedroom for $50 a month. He's divorced and his kids are grown, so he lives alone.

Before Walt lived in this house, my best friend Chuck lived there. I met Chuck Steinmiller in 1959 when I was four and he was seven. We have been friends ever since. We both love baseball and Roberto Clemente.*

During the week, I stop by my grandma's house again.

> Grandma, I saw that talking doctor and he thinks he can help me with my back. I am supposed to see him again on Friday.
>
> OK. But, please, no mention anything to your dad.
>
> I won't.

I give her the change from the $100 she had given me and she gives it right back.

> Here, you take this.

She hands me another $50.

> I hope-a he can help you.
>
> I think he can, Grandma. He's helped other people with my problem.

***

I couldn't wait to see Dr. Shoemaker again. I'm counting down the days.

* Clemente was a Pittsburgh Pirates baseball star named to the Baseball Hall of Fame in 1973.

On Friday at 4:30, I'm sitting in Dr. Shoemaker's waiting room. I never want to be late. Today I bring my book by Dr. Rubin with me. I want to show it to him. At 5 o'clock, his door opens. He smiles as he motions me to come in.

Hey, Lou. Another nice day outside.

Yeah. Dr. Shoemaker, here is seventy-five dollars.

I put it on his desk. He pushes the money aside.

Thank you. Lou, would you like some tea?

OK.

While he's getting the tea for me, I look all around his room. I see books everywhere. Most of them were written by Sigmund Freud.

Wow, you must really be smart. You've read all these books?

He smiles and pours my tea. I think he can tell that I'm impressed with him.

So you know all of the stuff in these psychology books?

It's all bullshit.

What?

All these books. They're all bullshit.

How can you say that? You're a medical doctor. I've been reading about guys like you.

What have you read?

Well, I know that you can prescribe medicine. That you are a psychoanalyst, which means that you've been on the couch yourself. You've been analyzed.

He smiles.

How do you know all of that?

I've been reading this book.

I show Dr. Rubin's book to him. He takes it and looks at it.

Yeah, I've heard of this guy.

I've read the whole book three times now.

Really?

Yes. I've learned so much.

Like what?

That people who have a lot of problems most likely have them because their parents screwed them up.

He nods. I can tell he is listening intently to every word I say.

The more I read this book, the more I know I need to see someone like you.

Why?

Because this doctor writes about his patients and he tells about their problems. He shows how their problems started in their childhood. His gives examples of how these people were treated as kids and how all of their problems stem from mistreatment by their parents.

He's looking right at me and taking in every word I say.

Dr. Shoemaker, I'm in deep trouble.

Why?

Because my dad treated me a hundred times worse than the people in that book.

What did he do?

He told me every single day that I was a bum and a jerk and that I would never amount to anything. EVERY DAY.

When did that start?

I know exactly when it started: February 2nd, 1966.

How did you remember the exact date?

Because that was the day my mom sent me from California to Pittsburgh. I was ten-and-a-half years old.

Tell me about that.

My mom and dad divorced when I was about two. My mom moved to Los Angeles when I was six. I stayed with my dad who lived with his mom and dad. He still does. After third grade, I begged my dad to let me visit my mom. He didn't want me to go, but he finally agreed as long as I promised to only stay the summer. Well, I liked it so much out there, I stayed. I lived in California in 1964 and 1965—fourth and fifth grades. During those two years, I made all As in school and was president of my fourth-grade class. My girlfriend

Susie Marco was vice-president of our class. Then my mom sent me back to my dad on February 2nd, 1966.

Why?

Because her second husband, Clyde, tried to molest me.

Dr. Shoemaker lights up a cigarette. I can't believe he's letting me talk this much. I can tell by the way he looks at me that he's taking in every word I'm saying.

What did he do to you?

He tried to touch me in my private area.

What did you do?

I pushed his hand away. He asked me if I knew how babies were made. I told him no, I didn't.

What else did he do?

Nothing.

Nothing else?

No.

I wonder why?

I think he was afraid I would tell my mom on him if he did. He told me not to tell my mom and I didn't for about six months.

You told her later?

Yeah. Only because she heard from a neighbor that Clyde was gay. My mom asked me on February 1st if he had ever tried to touch me. I told her the truth. She immediately confronted him. He denied it, of course.

Then what happened?

My mom called my dad and told him what happened. This was a Tuesday night. On Wednesday morning, I was flying home to Pittsburgh.

The very next day?

Yeah. I didn't even say goodbye to my friends.

He shakes his head and winces.

That must have been tough.

I was shocked. And something else happened to me the summer before. It was the summer of 1965 and I was almost ten years old.

What was that?

Our next door neighbor, a friend of our family, had become my piano teacher. She was married, about 25 years old, quite attractive. Before we knew it, instead of giving me lessons, we ended up kissing each other and falling in love. I would sneak over to her place every day and kiss with her on her couch.

How long did this go on?

About three months.

How did it end?

My mom walked in one day without knocking and caught us kissing on the couch. She started screaming and yelling at me. It scared the hell out of me.

That's *terrible*.

And there's more. This woman, Joanie, said she wanted to divorce her husband and marry me. It made me feel important having a grown woman *like* me the way Joanie did. She was willing to get a job and support me and marry me until I got out of high school.

When did she say that?

The evening that my mother found us. She insisted Joanie and her husband come over and tell us everything. I can still hear my mother yelling at me about this. Then six months later, the incident with Clyde happened. That's when my mother sent me off to Pittsburgh for good. I didn't want to leave California.

What happened when you got to Pittsburgh?

My dad wanted to kill me.

Why?

Because I had stayed in California for two and a half years and I was only supposed to go out there for three months.

Didn't he care that a grown man tried to molest you?

I shake my head no.

If he did, he never told me.

I could tell as soon as I walked off the plane that my dad hated me. My grandfather was with him and he hated me, too. All the way home in the car, they screamed at me. The ride from the airport to Carnegie is about thirty minutes, but it seemed like thirty hours. I cried the whole way. That was nine years ago. They have been humiliating and putting me down every day since then. Look at my fingernails. I bite them until they bleed. I don't even have nails anymore.

He looks at them and I can see his brain taking in all of this. I can tell he's on my side. *Finally* someone understands me.

Let me give you an analogy of what my life has been like.

The doctor looks right at me waiting to hear.

I felt like a little puppy dog living in a cage with two mean pit bulls. Every time the pit bulls would see me, they would attack and bite me. So I tried to avoid them as much as I could.

How did you avoid them?

I would hide up in my room so they wouldn't see me. All I would do is listen to the Beatles and read about Roberto Clemente. Dr. Shoemaker, I don't think I'm going to make it.

What do you mean?

I'm afraid of everyone.

Who are you afraid of?

EVERYONE. I've never been allowed to have any friends.

Any friend I tried to bring home, my family hated. I'm afraid of girls. I doubt if I'll ever get married. I've never had sex. I'm doomed.

Is there anything you've done in your life that you are proud of?

Yeah. I was a good baseball player in high school.

You liked baseball?

I loved baseball. I also learned to fly.

You did?

Yeah.

Did you solo?

Yes. I also got my licenses.

Private pilot?

Yeah. Plus I continued on and got my commercial license, instrument rating, multiengine rating, and flight instructor rating. All in six months. It normally takes years to get those.

He nods.

You've never mentioned this.

I haven't?

No.

I wonder why?

I shrug.

It's no big deal.

I disagree.

You do?

Yes.

Why?

Well, it takes a lot of work to accomplish all of that.

You think so?

Yes.

You're not just saying this to try and make me feel good?

No, Lou. I think it is an incredible accomplishment. Even more so considering your home life.

Dr. Shoemaker, can I tell you a story?

Of course, Lou.

On August 8th last year, a man told me that I'd never become a pilot. I know that date well because Richard Nixon announced that night on TV he would resign the next day— on August 9.

Dr. Shoemaker leans forward to listen intently.

I'd seen an ad on TV and went to meet with this guy who has a truck driving school. He was pressuring me to sign up for classes right away. I hesitated. I didn't really know what I wanted. So I said, "I'm still thinking that maybe some day I can become a pilot. I've passed all my tests so far." And you know what he *said* to me?

What?

"Son, you ain't *never* gonna become no pilot! You'd best get your ass in this truck-driving school and be happy about that."

I'm sorry to hear that, Lou.

So you can tell that I'm pretty screwed up and that my home life was really bad?

It was more than bad.

It was?

Yes.

Dr. Shoemaker, can I ask you a question?

He nods.

Do you have any kids?

Yes. I have four.

Did you ever call one of them a bum or a jerk?

Heavens, no.

Why not?

Why should I?

What do you call them?

What do you mean?

Like, if you need them for something.

I call them by their name.

Really?

Yes. One son is named Bob and the other is John. Doesn't your dad call you Lou?

No.

What does he call you?

Hey you. Hey asshole. Hey Angelo.

He shakes his head and winces. I love the fact that he seems to understand what I went through.

That's bad, huh?

He again shakes his head in agreement.

Do your kids call you Dr. Shoemaker?

No, they call me *Dad*.

They do?

Yes. What do you call your dad?

I don't call him anything. I try to never talk to him.

What do you mean?

Well, whatever room he is in, I leave. I try my best to avoid him.
So, your kids call you Dad?

Yeah. Sometimes they call me Asshole if I make them mad.

WHAT?

He smiles.

Yeah, sometimes I piss them off and they let me have it.

And you let them get away with that? Don't they know you are a MEDICAL DOCTOR?

Yeah, they know. They're not impressed.

They aren't?

No.

I'm impressed. Your kids need to have *my* dad. They're spoiled.

With that, I begin to cry.

Is that how normal people live?

Yes, Lou.

So you know that I was mistreated?

Yes.

I cry even harder. He pushes me a box of tissues on his desk.

Is there any hope for me?

Yes, I believe so.

Do you think you can help me?

I'll work as hard as I can, Lou.

CHAPTER 4
From Tuscany To Carnegie

"Appreciation can make a day, even change a life.
Your willingness to put it into words is all that is necessary."
- Margaret Cousins

During the next week, I moved my things down the street to my new place with Walt. He knows my situation from talking with Reba and Harold. I think he feels bad for me. His gas station is directly across the street from the house I grew up in, so he also knows my father and grandfather.

One afternoon, he tells me he wants to treat me to dinner at a local diner. This kind of takes me off guard. Why would he want to have dinner with me? His offer makes me nervous, but I had no time to think of an excuse to get out of it. He's around my dad's age and about the same built—5'11" maybe 220 pounds. I try my best to converse normally with him at dinner, but I'm scared to death. What do I talk about with an older guy? I'm clueless. Plus, it's painful to see a grown man trying to befriend me. Doesn't he know I'm worthless?

Our 45-minute meal feels like torture for me. When we finish, I'm so drained, I go straight to bed. I don't care that it's still light outside.

What's wrong with me? I see that other guys my age get along with older men. Why can't I? I bet Dr. Shoemaker can help me understand why.

Dr. Shoemaker, the man who let me live in his spare bedroom took me out to dinner last night.

That was nice of him.

Yes, it was, except that I could hardly talk to him.

He nods and takes a drag off his cigarette.

I felt so uncomfortable at the dinner. What's wrong with me?

Lou, I think you've been mistreated for so long that when someone treats you with respect, you feel unworthy.

So, people are supposed to treat me with respect?

That's normal, Lou.

I put my head in my hands and stare down at the floor.

What am I going to do? How can I get better?

Keep talking, Lou. You're doing fine.

How come you aren't taking any notes? In all the movies I've seen, the psychiatrists take notes.

That's because they're nervous.

How do you remember everything?

I remember. I'm taking it all in.

You really haven't said very much. How am I going to get better if you don't tell me what to do?

The more you talk, Lou, the more I'm learning about you.

So you're learning about me?

Yes. Tell me more about your family.

I've been living with my dad and his mom and dad, my
grandma and grandpap. Her name is Ada and his is Luigi.
They are both from Tuscany, Italy. My grandfather was born
in 1896 and moved to Carnegie in 1915. He had to leave
Italy because he almost killed a guy and the police were after
him. He knew a guy who had moved from his town in Italy
and settled near Bridgeville (Bridgeville is four miles from
Carnegie.) My grandfather moved in with this guy Pete and
his wife Yolanda. Yolanda had a picture of her sister on the
wall and my grandfather liked looking at it. Yolanda said,
"That's my sister. You like her?" He said, "Yeah" so she asked
him if he would like to marry her. He said "Yeah" again, and
they wrote her a letter telling her to get on the next boat. She
was only 14 and living in an orphanage in Massa Carrara. So,
he pretty much married her just from a picture. The fact that
they all came from the same town in Tuscany was a big deal.

My grandparents had three kids. Mary was born in 1920, my
dad was born in 1922, and my aunt Ann was born in 1925.
The two daughters got married young and my dad got married to my mom when he was thirty-three. He was the last
one to get married. He lived at home up until the day he
married my mom. Even then, he kept all of his clothes at his
parents' house and ate most of his meals with them. My dad's
family never really liked my mom. She was eleven years
younger than him and she wasn't Italian. The fact that she
was Irish made it even worse. My grandparents wanted him
to marry an Italian like his sisters did.

I take it your family didn't like Irish people?

They pretty much hate everyone except Italians. They

especially hate Jewish, Irish, and French people, although my grandfather likes Germans because he liked Hitler.

He liked Hitler?

Yeah.

Why?

Because Hitler killed a lot of people. My grandfather liked that. My grandparents never really learned to read or write. They still speak in broken English. My grandfather worked in the steel mill from the age of twenty until he retired in 1960 at the age of sixty-five. My grandma never worked outside of the home. She never learned to drive. You want to hear a good story?

Yeah.

When my grandma got off the boat in New York, she had to take a train to Carnegie. Well, she of course spoke no English. She found her way to the train station in New York and tried to find someone to help her get on the right train. She approached a train conductor and tried to tell him she wanted to go to CA-NA-GIA-PA. Well, the conductor has no idea what she meant. "Lady, I have no idea what you're saying." She showed him her papers and he read CARNEGIE, PA. "Oh, you want to go to CARNEGIE, PENNSYLVANIA?" "Yes, Yes, Yes," she nodded her approval. The conductor escorted her to the right train.

I can tell Dr. Shoemaker is enjoying this story. He's smoking away and drinking his tea.

That's a great story, Lou. Would you like some tea?

OK.

He pours me and himself some tea. I tell him I've got another good story if he'd like to hear it.

Yes, Lou. You're doing great.

Is this helping you to learn about me?

Very much so.

Well, after my grandparents got settled in Carnegie, my grandma wanted to start cooking for her new husband. So she took a bus to the store and tried to ask the salesman for something she needed. He, of course, didn't speak Italian and she could hardly speak two words of English. "Ma'am, what is it that you want?" "I want buy WATER-GO, MACA-RONI-STOP." "What?" "WATER-GO, MACARONI-STOP." He called over another salesman to see if he could figure it out. "What do you want, ma'am?" "I want WATER-GO, MACA-RONI-STOP." This went on for quite a while. Finally, another salesman showed her something on a shelf. "Is this what you want?" "YES, YES, YES." It was a colander.

Dr. Shoemaker laughs out loud. He likes that story, too.

CHAPTER 5
August 7, 1971: My Dream Is Born

"To fly, you must have resistance."

- Maya Lin

Lou, how did you become interested in becoming a pilot?

My mom came to see me in July, 1970. She visited Carnegie for two weeks and stayed with Reba and Harold. I hadn't seen her since February 2nd, 1966. While she was in town, we took a bus downtown to see the movie "Airport," starring Dean Martin. That movie made me want to become a pilot. In fact, I told my mom as we left the movie, "Someday that will be me, Mom. I'm going to become an airline pilot." She was great; she told me I could do it.

A year passed and then something big happened. My best friend, Tom Palombi, invited me to his cousin's 16th birthday party. I'll never forget the date: Saturday, August 7th, 1971. I had turned sixteen three days earlier. His party was held at the bowling alley in Carnegie. His name was Frank Palombi, and everyone at the party was congratulating him for soloing an airplane earlier that day.

Tom introduced me to Frank and I asked him what soloing meant. He said he had flown an airplane all by himself.

WHAT?

I flew an airplane by myself today.

You're kidding?

No, I really did.

Where?

At Campbell's Airport in Bridgeville.

I'd never heard of the place.

How did you do that?

I took lessons.

How many?

Fifteen.

Were you scared?

No, not at all.

Do you want to be a pilot someday?

Yeah. I want to fly for the airlines.

Well, that did it. I had met someone who did what I had only dreamed about. I got his phone number and learned more from him about Campbell's Airport and the flying school. I graduated from high school in May, 1973, and immediately began taking flying lessons there.

After saying all this to Dr. Shoemaker, I wait for his response.

Did your family know?

NO. NO WAY. I had saved up money and took enough lessons until I could solo in about two weeks.

Then what happened?

I went home and told my family.

How did they react?

They went CRAZY. You have to remember they are Italian immigrants who have never been outside of Carnegie. My dad went crazy because *his* dad got him all worked up about it.

But your dad came around?

Yeah.

How?

I begged and pleaded with him. I told him I could do it and that this is what I really wanted in life. I also got Frank Palombi's dad to talk to my dad, and got Reba and Harold to talk to him, too.

So your dad paid for all your lessons?

Yeah. Wait until you hear that story.

I'm listening.

First, he couldn't believe that I actually soloed a plane without him finding out. He wanted to visit this flight school to see what it was all about. So I arranged a meeting between him and the owner of the flight school, Sonny Clark. Sonny was also a pilot with TWA. He was based in New York at JFK and flew 747s from New York to the West Coast. This guy was impressive. He was about six foot four and two hundred ten pounds. He looked like a movie star. My dad almost wet himself when he met him. I think my dad was intimidated. Well, Sonny proceeded to tell him that I was a good student, and then had some of my instructors talk to my dad, too. They all told him I had the potential to become a pilot someday.

My dad is gruff. He has no tact—like a bull in a china shop. He has always embarrassed me everywhere we went. I was a nervous wreck because I knew he was going to embarrass me again. He did. He went from being intimidated by everyone at the school to being demanding.

My dad asked Sonny: How much money is involved for my kid to become one of these big-shot pilots?

Well, he will need to get his private pilot license. That will cost $4,000.

WHAT? YOU'RE CRAZY. YOU MUST BE KIDDING ME!

Then he will need to get his commercial pilot's license. That will cost $7,000.

YOU'RE NUTS. WHO DO YOU THINK YOU'RE TALKING TO? I WASN'T BORN YESTERDAY.

I was standing next to both of them and wanted to run away. I couldn't take much more of this. Then Sonny told my dad that I'll also need to get an instrument rating, multiengine rating, and flight instructor license.

My dad demanded: JUST GIVE ME THE COST OF THE WHOLE THING. ITEMIZE IT AND I'LL LOOK IT OVER. I

DON'T HAVE TIME TO WASTE WITH YOU PEOPLE. LET ME KNOW WHEN YOU COME UP WITH THE FINAL FIGURE.

Dad stormed off in a huff and I could see all of the flight instructors and secretaries looking at each other in shock. I was so embarrassed.

Dr. Shoemaker ponders this story in silence for a few moments.

Then what happened?

Sonny sent him an itemized statement that came to about $30,000. My dad went out to the airport and said: HOW MUCH WILL YOU TAKE OFF THIS IF I PAY THE WHOLE THING RIGHT NOW?

Are you saying you want to pay for everything up front?

YEAH.

My dad dickered back and forth with Sonny until he dropped the price way down and then my dad wrote him a check for the whole thing.

Lou, what does your dad do for a living?

I never told you?

No.

Oh man. Wait until I tell you . . .

CHAPTER 6
Living With Insanity

"When the giver comes, the door opens by itself."
- German Proverb

Have you ever eaten sausage?

Dr. Shoemaker nods *yes* as he sits back in his chair and puffs a cigarette.

Well, my dad owns a sausage-casing plant.

Where?

In Carnegie. It's located between Glendale and Cubbage Hill. It's hard to find because there are no paved roads to the plant. My dad used to be a salesman there. He did so well that he took over the company. There are about thirty employees. Most of them are Italian and can barely speak English. I started working there when I was in tenth grade. Do you know anything about a sausage-casing plant?

Not really.

Oh my God. It's the most disgusting place you've ever seen.

Why?

It stinks. It's gross. The smell gets on your skin and you can't get it off. Forget about your clothing. You pretty much have to burn your clothes to get rid of the smell. After I'd get home from work, I would immediately take a bath. If I went anywhere near people, they would look at me and say "you stink."

Here's how the business worked: These eighteen-wheel, air-conditioned trucks showed up with gigantic barrels on them. We used a forklift to take the barrels off the truck. Inside these barrels were pigs' intestines packed in salt. Well, we took all of these disgusting intestines and rinsed them in hot water to get the salt off and loosen them up. Then they had to be stretched apart. This was done on special sticks that were wide and smooth. Then we put the stretched-out intestines on big pallets. Each pallet held about three hundred sticks, which are actually stretched-out guts. Then these pallets went into gigantic dryers. The dryers held about twenty pallets. Do you know how much pigs' intestines in a dryer smells?

Dr. Shoemaker shakes his head *no*.

Believe me, you don't want to know.

After the guts dry, they have to be cut off the sticks by hand with a sharp knife. After being cut off, they are sewn together by ladies using a sewing machine. They are then packed in big barrels with salt and shipped to companies like Hormel. A lot of these guts are also used to go over salami.

Believe me, Dr. Shoemaker, this is one of the nastiest places on earth. You should be there on days when they interview people. They would put an ad in the paper looking for work-ers and then set aside one day a week to interview people. About 50 people would show up with no idea about the job. Most would walk in the plant for the interview and run out right away holding their noses. I've seen people actually

vomit when they came in. I never saw a black person even
want to fill out an application. They'd all run out holding
their noses. Do you want to hear a good one?

Yeah.

One black lady ran out of the plant holding her nose and she
yelled out, "KISS MY ASS. I'D GO ON WELFARE BEFORE
I'D EVER WORK HERE."

My friend Tom Palombi worked there in the summer of 1970
with me. My other friend, Chuck Steinmiller, wouldn't come
near the place.

Most of the employees disliked my dad. He only paid them
minimum wage unless they had been there for a long time.
Plus, he told them that if they tried to form a union, he
would close the place down immediately. They also hated the
way he treated me there. He was constantly yelling at me. I
could never do anything right.

They used to have a cat in the plant to keep away mice. One
day the cat walked in front of my dad and he kicked it across
the room. He almost killed it. One of the workers yelled at
my dad and asked, "What's your problem, don't you like
cats?"

Do you know what his answer was? "I HATE ALL
ANIMALS."

My dad worked seven days a week. In the evenings, he
would give music lessons. He had played the accordion since
he was a kid and he also taught others how to play it. He
gave lessons in the house on Saturdays and Sundays. Some
weekends, he played at weddings with his polka band. He
never sat still. He rarely watched television because he was

hard of hearing.

When he was about ten years old, he had developed scarlet fever and he almost died. That's how he lost his hearing. Because of his hearing loss, he never went to a movie theater and he was kept out of the military. There's only one TV show he watches religiously: wrestling. He and my grandpap go nuts over wrestling. They watch it every Saturday afternoon. They love the wrestler Bruno Samartino because he's Italian. You should see them when wrestling is on. They go crazy. They yell and scream at the TV. They act like a bunch of nuts. They have a feeling that the bout might be "fixed" but they don't care. They love it.

One day when I was about eight years old, I was watching a movie. My dad came in, sat down, and demanded to know what I was watching. I told him "The Wizard of Oz." Guess what he said?

I'm listening.

He said: "What's that?" He had never heard of that movie.

I can tell that Dr. Shoemaker is taking in every word I say.

Every morning before school, I would have to sit at the breakfast table with my dad and listen to him put me down. He'd say, "WHY EVEN GO TO SCHOOL? YOU'RE NEVER GOING TO AMOUNT TO ANYTHING ANYWAY. YOU MIGHT AS WELL JUST GO ON WELFARE AND GET IT OVER WITH. YOU'RE HOPELESS. YOU'RE A BUM. YOU'RE A JERK."

When did he start talking like this?

When I came back to Carnegie from California, halfway

through fifth grade. Every morning before school, I heard that. Get a load of this: I had to get up one hour early to hear this. I didn't have to get up until seven but he would be downstairs between five and six. To keep peace in the house, my grandparents made me get up and sit at the table with him. They weren't even up yet. My grandma would hear him downstairs, come in my bedroom, wake me out of a sound sleep, and say, "Louie, get up. Your dad is downstairs. Go sit with him."

Why did you have to sit with him?

Because he hated seeing me sleep. If I got up with him, it showed that I wasn't lazy. It showed that I had ambition like him. After he yelled at me, he would leave for work and then I could go back to bed.

Dr. Shoemaker shakes his head as though hearing this pains him.

Lou, I don't know how you were able to go to school.

A lot of time I didn't. In high school, I had a car and I drove to school. Many times I felt so ashamed, I would drive to the parking lot at South Hills Village Mall and sleep in my car. I just couldn't face people.

The only things that kept me going were baseball and Roberto Clemente. I played baseball in minor league, little league, and high school. I was a good hitter and a good pitcher. My grandpap would drive me to little league games. He even watched me play. He would sit next to the Civitarese family in the stands. Dr. Civitarese's son, Frank, was my age and we played all the way through high school together. Frank and I were two of the best players and my grandpap really admired his dad. His dad was one of the head surgeons at Allegheny General Hospital. Have you ever heard of his dad?

Yeah, I know who he is.

They were the nicest family. They never missed our games.
His dad was really into sports. He would rearrange opera-
tions so he could see Frank play. Can you believe that?
Besides being a surgeon, he was the high school sports doctor and he also worked at pro wrestling matches as the ring-
side doctor. My grandpap loved that. He'd sit in the stands at
my little league games with him and a few hours later, he'd
see him on TV when he watched wrestling. I remember
when Muhammad Ali came to Pittsburgh to fight in an exhi-
bition match. Dr. Civitarese examined him and his opponent.
In his home, there's a photo of the doctor with Muhammad
Ali.

Even Frank's mom would come to all of our games.
Sometimes when my grandpap couldn't take me, the
Civitarese family would pick me up in their station wagon.
They were so nice to me. They were nothing like my dad. I
wanted so bad to live with them. When they would drop me
off at home, I would go up to my room and cry. That's how
much I wanted to be around them.

CHAPTER 7
Getting My License, Losing My Hero

"If there be any truer measure of a man than by what he does, it must be by what he gives."

- Robert South

Dr. Shoemaker continues to probe about my father.

Did your dad ever hit you?

One time. It was Thursday, February 3rd, 1966.

How do you remember the exact date?

Because it was the day after I came back from California.

What happened?

My friend Robbie Johnson and I went outside to sled. It was a snow day so we didn't have school. As we walked down Noblestown Road with our sleds, Robbie threw a snowball at a truck and the snowball went through the side window. The truck stopped and the driver got out. Robbie said, "Lou, let's get out of here." I wasn't going to run because *he* did it, not me. Well, Robbie took off running and the driver walked right up to me and said, "You son of a bitch," and he punched me in the mouth. I fell onto the street. The driver calmly walked back to his truck and took off. I was in shock and my lip started bleeding. I start crying and yelled at the guy as he walked away. "I DIDN'T DO IT. THE OTHER KID

DID!"

Then what happened?

I ran home crying. Everyone was there: Grandpap, Grandma, and Dad. I ran into the house crying and started telling them what had happened. Well, they didn't even let me explain. They only heard that some truck driver punched me. That's all they needed to hear. They figured that I must have been causing trouble so they went absolutely crazy. My dad and grandfather attacked me. My dad punched me in the face and stomach, and knocked me across the floor. My grandfather grabbed me and lifted me back up, then my dad punched me in the face again. I was in total shock at this point. I yelled for them to stop and I tried to tell them that I didn't do anything wrong. They didn't hear me and didn't *want* to hear me. All they knew was that I must be guilty of something bad if a truck driver hit me. I screamed my head off at them. Before I knew it, my dad lifted me above his head, carried me upstairs, threw me on his bed, and slammed the door. He said I should have stayed in California with my mom. When he got back downstairs, I heard my grandfather yelling about how terrible I was. "I TOLD YOU HE WAS A BUM. WE OUGHT TO SHIP HIM BACK TO HIS MOTHER. YOU SHOULD HAVE NEVER TAKEN HIM BACK. I TOLD YOU HE WAS NO GOOD."

Dr. Shoemaker is listening intently.

Dr. Shoemaker, get a load of this—about five minutes later, the doorbell rang. It was a neighbor who saw the whole thing. He told my dad and grandfather that Robbie threw the snowball and that I did nothing wrong. He saw the guy punch me and drive off. He then got in his car, followed the truck, and got close enough to write down the license number on the truck. He even found out who the guy works for.

Then he gave my dad all of the information and told him he'd witnessed the whole thing. He said he would testify in court if my dad decided to sue. Guess what? We went to court and Robbie even confessed in front of the judge. The truck driver and his attorney decided to settle and my dad ended up with a thousand dollars. But he never even apologized to me.

That's unbelievable, Lou.

My grandfather always told me when I went outside to play, "If you break your arm, don't come home because we'll break the other one."

Dr. Shoemaker winces and shakes his head.

This is great—I'm finally telling my story of living in hell to someone who gets it! This is an incredible feeling.

Lou, what was your dad's childhood like?

All I know is what my grandma and aunts told me. My grandma told me never to ask my dad about his childhood. He hated talking about his past. I really can't imagine my dad even *being* a kid.

What did they tell you about his childhood?

The main story I remember was when my dad was about eight years old. He was supposed to get a haircut but he didn't want to get one because the barber cut his hair like a soup bowl—kind of like Moe's from the Three Stooges. Well, my grandfather got so mad that he beat my dad until he almost died. When my grandma told me that story, I asked my dad's sisters about it. They both got white in the face and were visibly shaken, just remembering it. My aunt Ann told me it was horrible. She remembered it like it was yesterday. My grandma really thought that my dad was going to die. She was afraid to call a doctor because she knew the authorities would arrest my grandpap. She ended up praying and saying the rosary so my dad would live. My grandfather beat my aunts, too. I was told that, when they were young, their job was to wash the dishes after dinner. One time they fought about who would wash and who would dry. Do you know what my grandpap did?

What?

He grabbed them both by the hair and beat their heads against the wall.

Dr. Shoemaker shakes his head in disbelief.

Also, my dad and grandpap were really cheap. My dad never bought new clothes or shoes. If I ever walked out of a room and didn't turn out the light, there would be a major blowup in the house. They would also never throw away pens even if they ran out of ink, so there were never any pens in the house that worked.

I wonder, Lou, how you got him to pay for your flying lessons.

I don't know. It was a miracle. He made me suffer for every lesson I took. I'll never forget when I passed my first license and became a private pilot.

What happened?

It was Saturday, August 4th, 1973, my eighteenth birthday. I had to fly a Cessna 150 down to Waynesburg, Pennsylvania, to pick up the FAA inspector who would give me my flight test. His name was Floyd Stockdale. He was about sixty years old and very nice. I picked him up and we flew around for about two hours. I had to perform several maneuvers for him. When the flight was over, he shook my hand and said, "Congratulations, you passed. You are now a private pilot." That meant I was now allowed to take people with me in the plane. I was so happy and proud of myself. I flew the plane back to Bridgeville and all of my instructors were happy for me. They all shook my hand and made a fuss over me. Well, I drove home to my house in Carnegie to tell my dad, grandma, and grandpap. Guess what my dad said?

What?

He said, "BIG DEAL. ANYONE CAN FLY ONE OF THOSE PUDDLE JUMPERS. GIVE ME THREE LESSONS AND I COULD DO IT."

So what did you do?

I went to bed. It was only about five o'clock and still light outside, but I went to bed anyway. I didn't even eat the cake that my grandma had baked for me. It actually seemed as though my dad was angry with me for passing. I think deep down he was hoping I would fail. The next day, I cried all day.

Why?

Because on Sunday, August 5th, Roberto Clemente was put into the Baseball Hall of Fame. He was only the second player in history that didn't have to wait the normal five years to be enshrined into the Hall of Fame. The only other player that baseball did this for was Lou Gehrig. My hero was now immortal. He died trying to help other people and now he was really gone. My dad saw me watching this on TV and

67

crying. Do you know what he said?

What?

He said, "THAT NIGGER WAS NEVER ANY GOOD. I
CAN'T BELIEVE THEY PUT HIM IN THE HALL OF FAME."

I start crying as I recall the story. I put my head in my hands and
look down at the floor. Dr. Shoemaker pushes the box of Kleenex
toward me and I blow my nose. As I look up at him, I can tell that
he feels bad for me. This is the only time I ever saw his eyes tear up.

CHAPTER 8
My Money Runs Out, My Sessions End

"Blessed is the influence of one true, loving soul on another."
- George Eliot

I arrive at Dr. Shoemaker's office with news.

> Dr. Shoemaker, my grandma told me she can't give me any
> more money to see you. My grandpap found out she was
> taking money out of the bank so I could pay you and all hell
> broke loose at home. My dad and grandpap are really letting
> her have it. She was crying and she told me I'd better stay
> away awhile. I've been bringing my bloody shirts to her and
> she's been washing them for me. The house I'm living in is
> only four houses down the street so I've been visiting her
> almost every day to say hi and eat lunch. Now I can't even
> do that. What am I going to do? I know I need to keep
> seeing you. You're the only person who has ever listened to
> me. I know I need help. What can I do?

> Lou, there is a clinic in Bridgeville you can go to. They only
> charge what you can afford. Since you're not making much
> money, they will see you almost for free.

He writes down the address and phone number for me.

> Do you really think they can help me?

> Yes. They have young therapists who are working on their
> PhDs and they are qualified.

I put my last $75 payment on his desk.

Dr. Shoemaker, I want you to know how much I appreciate you. You really seem to understand what I went through. Did I ever tell you that when I was in eleventh grade, I went to the police station to report my dad?

No, you never told me that.

Well, I did. I couldn't take it anymore, so I drove to the police station and asked the police if they could talk to my dad.

Did they?

Yeah, they came to the house. I thought my dad would get scared and start treating me better. It didn't work. You want to know why?

Yeah, what happened?

It turns out that one of the policeman's nephews takes accordion lessons from my dad. They ended up being buddy-buddy and the cop told me that my dad is a good man and that I should listen to him. Unbelievable.

Dr. Shoemaker shakes his head in amazement.

When my session is over, he walks me to the door and shakes my hand.

Good luck, Lou.

I start crying. I know Dr. Shoemaker could have helped me. He had been giving me hope. Now that hope is gone. However, something tells me I'll see him again.

CHAPTER 9
My New Therapist

"If you're going through hell, keep going."
- Winston Churchill

I know I need a lot of help and I don't want to waste any time. So the very next day, I call the Bridgeville Mental Health Clinic. Two days later, they call back and tell me they'd set up an appointment for me with a therapist named Kathy Graff.

I show up for my appointment 30 minutes early and the receptionist has me fill out some papers. After I finish, I wait to meet my new therapist, probably an older woman who was maybe my mother's age. I'm shocked when a young, beautiful young woman comes out and introduces herself as Kathy Graff. The first thing I notice is her age—not much older than me. The second thing I notice is how pretty she is—tall with brown hair and brown eyes.

Kathy greets me and invites me into a room that has only two lone chairs. Nothing in this room leads me to think it's her personal office.

For the next six months, I saw Kathy once a week in that empty room. I'd tell her a little about my life but nothing to the extent that I've told Dr. Shoemaker. Every week, all I wanted to do was learn more about *her*.

To me, Kathy is amazing. At 27 years old, she's earned her master's degree in psychology and is working on her PhD at the University of Pittsburgh. And she isn't married. I can't believe I'm actually sitting next to a "normal" person—a person going somewhere in life. She's going to become a DOCTOR. Wow.

All I can think about each day while working at the Holiday Inn is
Kathy. Sometimes at night, I cry in bed thinking about her. I want to
be like her. These are my continuing thoughts:

>I want to be normal.
>I wonder what it must be like to be normal.
>I bet her parents even *care* about her. Maybe they
>even *love* her.
>
>I want to have a good job.
>I want to be somebody.
>I want people to respect me.
>
>Who am I kidding? I'll never have those things. I'll never
>have a girlfriend. Who could possibly care for a person like
>me?
>
>I'm worthless.
>I'm a loser.
>I'll never amount to anything.
>I'm a bum.

Every time I'd hear the popular song "Sister Golden Hair" by
America, I'd think of Kathy. I want her to like me. But who was I kidding? She'd never like a guy like me. She probably has a real
boyfriend. One who is not afraid of everyone like I am. A guy who
has a really important job. I bet she even has sex. Wow, that's unbelievable.

I know I'm getting worse because of my deep infatuation for Kathy. I
begin saving my money so I can see Dr. Shoemaker again.

CHAPTER 10
Returning to Dr. Shoemaker

"Too often we underestimate the power of a touch, a smile, a kind word, a listening ear, an honest compliment, or the smallest act of caring, all of which have the potential to turn a life around."

- Leo Buscaglia

After about six months of seeing Kathy, I can't take my infatuation with her any more. I feel like I'm losing it. My only recourse, as I see it, is to contact Dr. Shoemaker again. Although I'm only making $280 a month at my job at the Holiday Inn, I've saved enough money for two more visits.

I dial Dr. Shoemaker's phone number, knowing that he always answers his own phone, even when he is seeing someone.

Hello.

Dr. Shoemaker?

Yes.

This is Lou Panesi. Do you remember me?

Yes, Lou.

Dr. Shoemaker, I have some money. Can I see you sometime?

I can tell he's looking at his appointment book.

Lou, can you come in next Tuesday at five o'clock?

Yes.

OK. I'll see you then.

Thank you, Dr. Shoemaker.

I can't wait to see him again. He is the one guy who knows me and understands me.

The following Tuesday, I enter his office and extend my hand to greet him. As we sit down, I put $75 cash on his desk.

Thank you for seeing me, Dr. Shoemaker. I went to that clinic you told me about.

That's good, Lou. How was it?

It was OK except that the therapist they gave me was young and beautiful. I've been seeing her for six months. She's all I think about. She's 27 and she has a master's degree and she's working on her PhD.

He nods without saying anything.

You should see her; she's *gorgeous*.

He begins to pour himself a cup of tea and offers me one, which I accept.

I canceled my last two appointments with her because I feel like I'm getting worse. I was seeing her once a week, but every time I saw her, it was torture. I even asked her if it was OK to have sex with her.

What did she say?

She said that she would have to ask her supervisor.

He lets out a slight laugh.

Really? Is that what she said?

Yeah.

He shakes his head in disbelief.

Dr. Shoemaker, do you think she actually has sex?

I have no way of knowing, but if she is 27 and working on her PhD, I would say that she is doing OK for herself.

Really? You really think that she has sex?

I would think so.

Wow, I think about her all day long. It's kind of driving me crazy. Do you think she makes a lot of money?

Not yet. Right now, she's just getting experience. When she gets her PhD, she'll do all right for herself.

She must be smart.

He nods. I can tell he's taking in everything I'm saying.

Do you know what I think, Lou?

What?

I think you wanted to fuck her brains out.

WHAT!!!!!

I almost fall out of my chair.

What did you say?

I think you wanted to fuck her brains out, Lou.

You think THAT?

Yeah.

Is that OK? I mean, isn't that *bad*?

Why is that bad?

You mean, if I ever had sex, you would still like me?

Why wouldn't I? Having sex is normal, isn't it?

Really?

Lou, you have to know that people *do* have sex, don't you?

I guess, but to me it's bad.

Lou, let me tell you something. She is an amateur.

She is?

It takes 30 years to learn how to do this.

So all therapists aren't the same?

Most therapists, in my opinion, can't find their ass with both hands.

Do you think that *you* are good?

In my mind, I'm as good as they come.

Wow, that makes me feel good. I saved up the money myself
to see you. I work 30 hours a week at the Holiday Inn and I
make $2.50 an hour so I make about $70 a week. My only
bills are my rent. I pay Walt $50 a month plus $50 a month
for utilities. Reba and Harold feed me almost every day and
that helps me. I want you to know that I have been reading a
lot of books on psychology and child rearing since I last saw
you. I've learned a lot...mostly that sickness travels from
generation to generation in people's families. All I know is
that I want this junk to end with me.

I pause.

Dr. Shoemaker, do all psychiatrists have the ability to do
what you're doing for me?

In my opinion, there are only a handful of psychiatrists in
the world who can do what I'm doing.

At that moment, I *know* I'm in the presence of a great doctor.

Can I ask you another question?

Sure.

So you can remember *everything* I'm telling you?

I remember everything, Lou.

Do you know what's wrong with me?

He puffs on his cigarette slowly and sips his tea. He seems to be putting me off, but I persist.

You want a diagnosis, don't you, Lou?

Yes.

He then spits out such a long, complicated diagnosis that I have no idea what he is saying. All I remember are the words "Oedipus complex" somewhere in all of what he said. But his words reassure me that he *knows* what's wrong with me. He knew what I wanted to hear; he stated it in a way that erased all worries from my mind.

But I have one more question. What about my back? What's *wrong* with my back? Why does it bleed all the time, Dr. Shoemaker?

In my opinion, Lou, your back is a psychosomatic illness caused from being your dad's whipping boy. It's also caused from having a lot of pent-up rage toward your dad inside you.

Really?

Yes.

So I really hate my dad?

How could you not?

I knew that I was afraid of him but I never knew I hated him. So my anger toward him that I have built up is causing my back to bleed?

Yes.

Can I be helped?

I believe so.

Do you know how to help me?

Yes.

What can *I* do?

Keep talking. You're doing great.

As I leave Dr. Shoemaker's office, I realize that I finally have an answer about my back. It's bleeding because I am my dad's "whipping boy" and because I have rage built up against him. Wow, I *finally* know the answer to that question. It was like the clouds parted and I could see the stars above.

Maybe there's hope for me after all.

CHAPTER 11
No Charge?

"We can discover this meaning in life in three different ways: (1) by doing a deed; (2) by experiencing a value; (3) and by suffering."

- Victor Frankl

After my visit with Dr. Shoemaker, I immediately go and tell my grandma that this doctor knows *exactly* what is causing my back to bleed and that he feels confident it can be "cured" with treatment from him. My grandma then begs my dad to pay for more visits to this "psychiatrist." My dad, of course, blows up and calls Dr. Shoemaker a quack. But a funny thing happens next. He actually agrees to pay this doctor a visit.

The visit takes place on Monday, May 31st, 1976—a Memorial Day holiday. I distinctly remember the date because Dr. Shoemaker is the only doctor working in his entire building that day. My dad has a one o'clock appointment and I have my session at two o'clock.

I can hardly believe that my dad is actually inside Dr. Shoemaker's office. Because no one's in the building, I feel free to put my ear to the doctor's door and listen to what they're talking about. I hear Dr. Shoemaker telling my dad that I'm afraid of him. My dad immediately rebuffs him by saying, "If that boy would just listen to me, I would give him my whole business someday."

I also hear Dr. Shoemaker raise his voice to get his point across to my dad. My dad pressures Dr. Shoemaker to tell him what I say when I visit him. Dr. Shoemaker firmly tells my dad, "That information is confidential." I'm blown away by that! Dr. Shoemaker is backing me and won't give in to my dad on that matter. That's so awesome. Here, I'm getting something I never got at home: respect.

Finally, as my dad's visit ends, I take my seat in the waiting room so they can't see that I've been eavesdropping. After my dad leaves, I go in to start our two o'clock session.

In that session, Dr. Shoemaker tells me that trying to change my dad is hopeless.

> Dr. Shoemaker, weren't you afraid of my dad?
>
> Me, afraid of your dad? Hell no. I would kick your dad's ass.
>
> Really?
>
> Yes. I was a boxer in the military and I beat up on guys a lot bigger than your dad.
>
> *NO WAY.*
>
> Yes way.

Hearing this excites me to no end. *Finally*, I meet someone who isn't afraid to stand up to my dad.

> Lou, let me tell you something. Your dad might be 55 years old but emotionally he is about 10. He was so abused by your grandfather at a young age that he never had a chance to grow up. Your dad is just a scared little boy in a man's body.

Wow, this blows my mind. My dad is really a frightened little boy. Incredible.

> Lou, your dad acts like a big man because he has a lot of

money. BIG FUCKING DEAL. Your dad is the fucking Gut King of Carnegie.

My mouth falls open.

Lou, don't get your hopes up on your dad paying for any more visits to see me.

Really?

Lou, here's why. Your dad is jealous of *me*. He wants you to idolize *him*, not me or Roberto Clemente.

Yeah, but I hate him.

I know you do. But if you knew how to handle your dad, you could have him wrapped around your finger.

I could?

Yes.

Please, tell me how.

Lou, you are all that your dad has in this world that is any good. If you could try and see the world through his eyes, he would give you *anything*.

You really think so?

Yes, I do.

Dr. Shoemaker, you know what my dream is?

What?

I want to return to Ohio University in the fall and then graduate. You know that I've already finished one year there. I only need three more.

Why didn't you continue?

My grades weren't good. I think my first year GPA was 1.8. Plus I was afraid of everyone. I felt like a 10 year old myself living with college students. I mean, one of my roommates was having sex all the time. That kind of freaked me out, being a virgin and all. I never made any friends. I was afraid of everyone there.

Lou, can you come back tomorrow?

Yes, except that I might not have enough money if my dad doesn't give me any.

I wouldn't count on him paying for this, Lou.

So, how am I going to *pay* you?

Let *me* worry about that.

I start crying uncontrollably.

Are you sure you want to get involved with a person like me? I'm a loser. You're too nice a guy to get involved with a bum like me. I'll end up ruining your life.

You let me worry about who I'll see and who I won't see. I'll see you tomorrow, Lou.

Okay.

As I walk out the door, I can't believe that Dr. Shoemaker is actually offering to see me at no charge.

CHAPTER 12
"You Need A Gimmick"

"There is a giant asleep in every man.
When the giant awakens, miracles happen."

- Frederick Faust

After I leave Dr. Shoemaker's office, all I can think of is what he told me about my dad.

To me, my dad is this big, domineering guy who intimidates the heck out of me. But to Dr. Shoemaker, he is just a scared little boy who still lives with his mommy and daddy. I mean, *Dr. Shoemaker isn't even afraid of my dad.* That really blows my mind.

Dr. Shoemaker is the kind of man I never knew existed. He seems to be a man's man. Smart, insightful, yet a fighter, too. He boxed in college and in the military. Clearly, he isn't a wimp like me.

As I drive away, I actually laugh out loud when I recall his words about my dad. "I could kick your dad's ass." That's one of the greatest things I'd ever heard in my life.

I start to feel something that I had never felt before—*sympathy for my dad.* According to Dr. Shoemaker, he had no chance at life. He grew up in the Depression during the 1930s and my grandfather used to beat him physically all the time. I begin to look at my dad differently. Maybe he *is* someone to be pitied. Maybe Dr. Shoemaker *is* right. If I could look at life through my dad's eyes, maybe I can rise above my feelings toward him and get along better with him.

My grandma invites me over for dinner that night. I know my dad will be there. I'm hoping for the best, but I'm prepared for the worst. Deep down, I'm hoping he liked Dr. Shoemaker and would pay for my visits.

I find out the answer soon enough.

We all sit down for dinner. Then my dad starts talking to my grand-pap.

> Yeah, Dad. I went and saw that quack today. He's a bum. They're all bums, Dad. You know as well as me that all they want is your money. I saw that clock on his wall keeping track of the time. He just wanted to soak me good, but I'm too smart for a guy like him.

My grandfather puts in his two cents with his broken English.

> Yeah, Louie, I no like-a doctors my whole life. You canna not trust any them. They all in it for da money.

Normally, I would have said something in defense of Dr. Shoemaker, but I remember what he told me about my dad, that he's jealous of my seeing him. So I don't waste my time saying anything.

Actually, that night, communication is slightly civil in the house because I don't argue with them. I think they expect that I will. I'm also sure not to mention that I'm seeing Dr. Shoemaker the next day. I know that will cause a war at the dinner table.

Later that night, I go back to my place feeling a little dejected. One part of me had hoped that my dad would encourage me to keep seeing Dr. Shoemaker. But at least now I know why he wouldn't—he's *jealous*. I love knowing that. It changes everything for me. I can't wait to see Dr. Shoemaker because I want to learn more from him.

The next day, I tell Dr. Shoemaker about the dinner.

Dr. Shoemaker, I had dinner at my grandparents' house last night and you were right about my dad. He called you a quack and said all doctors are full of shit and that they just want people's money. He refused to pay for the visit yesterday but my grandma gave me $75 to cover his visit. She told me that she cannot pay for any more visits because my grandpap is really watching the money. I think he is suspicious of her helping me. I don't know what to do. I don't make enough to keep seeing you but I know that I need you. Please don't send me back to Kathy and the clinic.

We'll work something out, Lou.

Really?

Yes. Let me worry about that. Tell me more about last night.

Well, actually I took your advice. I knew my dad was jealous of you so I didn't try to convince him of anything. I never told him I was seeing you today. If I did, there would have been a war in the house. I really appreciate your telling me about my dad. I never knew those things. I want to know everything *you* know. I need your help.

I'm glad you didn't get into a pissing contest with him last night because you know as well as I do that it would have been a losing battle, right?

I know. That's why I didn't do it.

Dr. Shoemaker pours himself and me some tea, then lights a cigarette.

Dr. Shoemaker, last visit you told me that if I knew how to

handle my dad that I could have him wrapped around my finger.

That's true.

Can you tell me how to do that?

Lou, take a look at your dad's life. He's really suffering. He doesn't have any friends; he never had an opportunity to get an education; he still lives in the small little town that he was born in; he never cut the cord from his mommy and daddy. In fact, he still basically lives with them, right?

Yes.

Some people would look at your dad as a pathetic soul. Plus the fact that he beats up on a poor, defenseless young boy, his only son. What's that tell you about him?

Do you think that he ended up this way because of the way my grandfather treated him when he was young?

Yes, of course, Lou. Your grandfather was a tough son of a bitch and he terrorized your dad when he was little. What did you tell me once, that he beat him when he was about 10 years old because he didn't want to get a haircut?

Yeah, according to my grandma and aunts, they all thought that my dad might die because the beating was so severe.

That's terrible, Lou. Think of what hell your dad had to go through. It doesn't mean that he should have mistreated you and what he did to you all those years was unforgivable. But you're all he's got. If you could find it in your heart to under-stand why he behaved the way he did—if you could become his equal and befriend him to some extent—your dad would give you anything.

But I don't want to work my whole life in the gut factory.

You won't have to. If you can get your anger out toward your dad in this office and appease him when you are around him, I think that you'll find he would pay for your return to college. I could be wrong, but I've got a good feeling about this.

You really think he would do that?

Yes, I do. Lou, let me tell you something. I went to high school with guys like your dad. The guys I hung out with all had pretty nice parents and a lot of my friends went on to college. Some of my childhood friends are now doctors. And I knew a lot of guys like your dad, too. They were the guys who majored in shop class and went on to be car mechanics and construction workers. There is nothing wrong with that, but those guys never had a chance to go to college.

Can I ask you a question, Dr. Shoemaker?

Yes.

Did you have good parents?

Yes.

They liked you?

They loved me.

They *LOVED* you?

Yes, of course. Do you see how you asked that? That's foreign to you. That just shows the kind of house that you grew up in. It was devoid of love and respect for each other.

Wow. Your parents *respected* you?

Yes.

They never called you a bum or stupid?

Heavens no. I never called my own kids that, either.

Were you allowed to have girlfriends?

Yes, of course.

And your parents were nice to them?

Yes, why shouldn't they be?

Man, this is so different than the way I was raised.

It's also different than the way *your dad* was raised.

Dr. Shoemaker, I have a question.

He nods and puffs on his cigarette.

I tried to make a conversation with a girl at the bank and it didn't go anywhere. She asked me what I did and I told her that I worked at the Holiday Inn. She just said "Oh" and that was pretty much it. The conversation died right off. I actually left the bank feeling embarrassed.

Lou, you need a gimmick.

A *what?*

A gimmick.

What's a gimmick?

It's something that people find interesting. A lot of people your age go to college. That's interesting and it leads to a lot of other questions like, "What is the school like? What are you majoring in?" That's a lot different than if you were a welder. Being a welder is a noble profession, but it doesn't seem interesting to people.

Wow, I never knew this stuff.

Dr. Shoemaker, do you think we could get my dad to send me back to Ohio University in the fall? That's what I really want to do.

Lou, can you come back on Monday?

Yes.

I'd like to start seeing you twice a week.

Dr. Shoemaker, are you sure? I won't be able to pay you.

I'll see you on Monday at four o'clock.

OK. Thank you very much, Dr. Shoemaker.

CHAPTER 13
"Do Men Your Age Kiss Women?"

"When a deep injury is done us, we never recover until we forgive."
- Alan Patton

The more I meet with Dr. Shoemaker, the more questions I have for him. I count the moments until our next visit. Again, I keep thinking of the things he said to me about my dad and about needing a gimmick.

I decide to keep away from my grandparents' house. I just work at my part-time job at the Holiday Inn and hang out with Reba and Harold. They're very nice to me. Reba invites me over every day for dinner. It's almost like I am their son. They even buy me clothing.

The weather during the spring and summer in Pittsburgh has been great. It seems like every day is warm and sunny. All we see on TV are stories about the upcoming presidential election in November. It will be Gerald Ford against Jimmy Carter.

When Monday arrives, I drive to Oakland through the University of Pittsburgh campus to see Dr. Shoemaker. Again, I make sure that I'm at least 30 minutes early—in case there's a traffic jam or something. I definitely don't want to be late.

I sit in the waiting room waiting for Dr. Shoemaker to open his door and greet me. I'm always nervous until he breaks the ice with me. He knows how to make me feel comfortable.

Dr. Shoemaker opens the door, gives me a nice smile, then tells me to come in.

Nice day outside, Lou.

Yes, the weather has been beautiful.

Would you like some tea?

OK.

As he pours me tea, I say . . .

Dr. Shoemaker, can I ask you a favor?

Sure, Lou, what is it?

When I sit in your waiting room, I'm always very nervous.
Whenever you open your door to greet me, I jump with fear
inside. Is there any way you could open your door slower for
me?

Yes, of course. I'm sorry if I startle you, Lou.

That's OK.

Lou, you can see how intimidated you have been of older
people your whole life.

It's not just older people. I'm pretty much afraid of everyone,
I think. I'm deathly afraid of my boss at the Holiday Inn. She
is a woman about 40 or 50 years old and I'm always afraid
that she will yell at me. She's the head of the housekeeping
department. The only friend I have is my co-worker. His
name is John Saittis and he's a lot like me. He's afraid of
everyone, too. His dad is just like my dad. He has put John
down his whole life, too. John smokes and you should see
his hand shake when he smokes. He can barely get the cigarette to his mouth. I think he must smoke three packs a day.

Dr. Shoemaker puffs on his cigarette and listens to me.

I was thinking about what you told me about gimmicks. I've never heard of that in my whole life. Did you study that in medical school?

Lou, it's just common sense.

It is?

Yes.

So Freud didn't write about that in all of his books on psychology?

No.

It's just real life, Lou. Everyone deep down wants to be respected, right? You don't realize it, but you have the greatest gimmick in the world.

I do?

Yes.

What's that?

You're a *pilot*. Girls like that. Everyone respects pilots. Look at how impressed your dad was with the guy who owned the flying school.

Yeah, he was really impressed with him. Part of it was that he was wearing his TWA uniform that day.

Girls also like a man in uniform, Lou.

You really think so?

Yes, of course.

My dream is to be like Sonny Clark and fly for the airlines, but first I have to become a college graduate.

Lou, I really think that your dad would send you back to Ohio University if you handled him right.

Tell me what to do.

It might take your being around him more, but I'm confident that you'll be able to handle your dad.

The other day when I went over for dinner, I didn't fight with my dad and grandpap about you. I think they figured I would.

That showed a lot of maturity on your part, Lou. Your dad is a sorry soul. You need to pray for that mother fucker. The poor guy is fucked up. Like we talked about before, he had no chance at life. All he wants in the world is for you to respect him. I know it's hard to do, but that's what he wants. If you could find it in your heart to understand that he's really a hurting person, if you could reach out to him, believe me, he would give you the world. When he was here last week, he told me that he would give you anything he had.

Yeah, as long as I work in the gut factory with him my whole life. But I don't want that.

Isn't there anything else you can do besides work in the sausage-casing plant?

Yeah. He also has a separate building where they make rubber stamps. It doesn't smell in there.

Do you think that you could work there until school starts? I
believe that he would pay for you to go back to college. You
might have to work with him until September.

I know he needs someone to help in that area because he
used to mention it to me before he threw me out of the
house.

You see, he would love that.

But I'm afraid that he'll end up yelling at me all over again.

Fuck him. He's an asshole. You're on a mission to get back to
school. You would work there for three or four months if it
could get you back to school, wouldn't you? Plus, I want to
see you twice a week during this time. Between you and me,
I know you'll get through this. Would you like more tea?

OK.

Just then the phone rings and he picks it up on the second ring. He
always picks it up on the second ring. It seems like someone is
making an appointment. He's on the phone for about a minute.

Dr. Shoemaker, can I ask you a question?

He nods yes.

Do men your age kiss women?

Yes. You know what else?

What?

We fuck, too.

WHAT! My eyes bug out and my mouth falls open. I can't even respond to that answer. I'm in shock.

> Why do you seem so surprised, Lou? Isn't that where you came from?

> I guess.

> Your parents had to fuck in order for you to be here, right?

I nod.

> The reason I asked you that is because I noticed that Jimmy Carter has a really young daughter and that made me wonder.

> Oh, Jimmy Carter fucks.

> You really think so?

> Sure.

> Doesn't that bother you?

> Hell no, why should it?

> I mean, he's the *president of the United States*.

> So what? He's a man first, right?

> I guess. You wouldn't be afraid of him if you met him?

> Fuck no. I'd shake his hand. I wouldn't be afraid of him.

> I don't think my dad fucks.

He probably doesn't. That's why he's fucked up. Do you think your dad eats pussy?

WHAT!!

Do you think your dad eats pussy?

NO WAY! I've never really seen him with a woman.

Oh, that could explain why he's so angry all the time.

I don't fuck. I've never fucked.

Your time will come, Lou.

You think so?

Yes, I do.

Wow, and you would still *like* me?

Why wouldn't I? My kids fuck.

They *do*?

Sure.

And that doesn't bother you?

Hell no. Why should it?

You don't try to stop them?

Of course not. How could I stop them? It's a normal act. Just like eating and shitting and farting. Everyone does it, right?

I let out a laugh. This guy is funny.

>I can't believe you're a psychiatrist. You don't talk like how I imagined one would talk. Are all psychiatrists like you?

>Like I told you before, in my opinion, most psychiatrists can't find their ass with both hands.

Wow, this guy is amazing.

>Lou, can you come back on Thursday at four o'clock?

>Yeah.

He writes out an appointment card and walks me to the door. I extend my hand to him to thank him for seeing me, even though I'm not paying him. My handshake is limp. I extend my hand meekly with the fingers pointed downward, almost like a dog extending its paw. It's one of the worst handshakes you can imagine.

As Dr. Shoemaker shakes my hand, he stops me.

>Lou, can I show you something?

>Yes.

>Can I show you how most men shake hands?

>OK.

>Here, grab my hand like you're shaking it.

I grab it.

>Now squeeze it firmly.

He shows me what he means.

> This is how men shake hands. Your handshake is very weak
> and a lot of men judge you by your handshake.

> Wow, I never knew that. I guess that's why everyone I shake
> hands with crushes my hand.

> I think that's why.

> Thank you for showing me that, Dr. Shoemaker.

> Lou, I hope you don't take offense to my showing you things
> like that.

> No. Not at all. Please tell me everything you know about
> everything. I like hearing this stuff.

CHAPTER 14
"You've Got To Be Ambidextrous"

"I advise you to say your dream is possible and then overcome all inconveniences, ignore all the hassles and take a running leap through the hoop, even if it is in flames."

- Les Brown

After I leave Dr. Shoemaker's office, my head is spinning. *Guys his age really have sex?* That seems unbelievable to me. I thought that only young people had sex—like people in dirty movies. I've never seen an older person in one of those types of movies. I wonder if Dr. Shoemaker has ever seen one of those movies. I need to ask him.

Plus, I finally have the answer to why guys crush my hand when they shake hands with me. *I'm supposed to squeeze back firmly.* Unbelievable.

I want someone to shake hands with so I can try out my new technique. When I go back to my house, Walt is there. So I go up to him, extend my hand, and thank him again for letting me stay in his house. I shake his hand just like Dr. Shoemaker showed me and it works. It actually makes me feel more like a real person. Before, I used to dread shaking men's hands because I always felt like a wimp afterwards.

I also start to think more about my dad. Dr. Shoemaker has again told me about how screwed up my dad is. He even asks if I want to "pray for that mother fucker" with him. I don't know if he's kidding about the praying. All I know is that it really makes me feel good. It tells me that he "gets it" about my dad. He knows for sure that my dad is a jerk.

The next day, I go to my grandma's house for lunch. While I'm there, my dad stops by. I decide to approach my dad with a request.

> Dad, I just wanted you to know that I won't be seeing that doctor anymore. He told me that you were a good man and that you only want the best for me. I just want to say I'm sorry if I have been ungrateful. It's only because I've been immature. If you still need someone to help make rubber stamps, I would like to help out.

This offer stops my dad in his tracks.

> I told that quack I would do anything for you if you only listened to me. I give him credit for telling you that. So, you're not going to keep seeing him, are you?

> Heck no. I think you were right, Dad. He may have only been in it for the money.

> No maybes about it. He definitely only wants people's money. I wasn't born yesterday. Can you come up to the plant tomorrow? I could use someone to help Evan with the stamp-making.

Evan is a 30-year-old single man who runs the rubber stamp division of my dad's business. A good guy, he pretty much hates my dad like everyone else but he tolerates him because of the steady job. He's one of the few people who isn't intimidated by my dad. At times, they really go at it with each other. Evan knows my dad is a mean SOB. My dad likes Evan because he's a great worker and he's very organized. He knows where everything is and keeps the place neat while my dad has his stuff around everywhere.

My job is to work with Evan making rubber stamps and name plates.

This is 100 times better than working in the gut factory, which is only 100 yards away.

My dad notices a difference in me and starts treating me better. He even takes me out to lunch with him. I always manage to edify him by telling him he is a great businessman. He eats this up because, finally, someone is telling him that he's smart. He especially likes it when I mention that he never had any help from **his** dad.

> Hell, no. My dad never gave me anything. All he ever taught me was to work.

> So you never had a dad like yourself?

> No, I didn't. If you listen to me, you could have everything that I've built.

> I appreciate that, Dad. I want to learn from you.

I make sure I never mention Dr. Shoemaker to my dad. If I do, I know it would ruin all of my chances to get back to school.

On my next visit to Dr. Shoemaker, I'm bursting with questions. But first I want to tell him how well things are going with my dad.

> Dr. Shoemaker, everything you told me to do is working perfectly. I'm getting along pretty well with my dad. He's even taken me out to lunch a few times. I try to edify him and make him feel good about himself.

> He doesn't get that very often, Lou.

> You're right. And you have to admit he has done well for himself, considering that no one ever helped him out.

> Your dad's money makes him feel equal to people who are educated.

I don't know this for sure, but I would guess that he's worth about a million dollars.

That's incredible when you think about it, Lou. And yet, he is a miserable bastard.

That's right, he is. I wonder why.

Lou, as I told you before, you are the only good thing in his life. If you could be his friend, he would do anything for you. Who *else* is he going to leave his money to?

I think you're right.

Would you like some tea?

OK.

He pours both of us cups of tea and lights a cigarette.

Dr. Shoemaker, I have a question.

Go ahead.

Have you ever seen an X-rated movie?

No, have you?

Yes.

His eyes brighten and he reacts like an excited kid.

Tell me, Lou, do they show *everything*?

Yeah.

You mean they even show it going in and out!?

Yes.

Wow.

How come you've never seen one of those movies? Everyone I know has seen them.

I don't have to watch other people fuck.

This shocks the hell out of me. *He doesn't have to watch other people fuck.* He must be kidding me. I think he can easily tell that I'm shocked at hearing that.

Lou, sex is supposed to be fun.

To me it's not.

That's because that asshole stepdad of yours tried to touch you when you were ten years old. That mother fucker should be in jail.

Really?

Yes.

That piano teacher, too. You've had some real crazy adults in your life. Almost every adult that you have come in contact with has messed with you. From what you've told me, only Reba and Harold have been good to you and treated you with respect. Your mom did at times, but she's fucked up, too.

And parents are important, according to all of those books I've read. Right?

Yes.

I've never really had an adult male be nice to me except for you.

* * *

In our sessions over the next three months, Dr. Shoemaker would lean back in his reclining swivel chair and tell me stories about how he and his sons would go fishing or big game hunting in Africa. Telling these stories would last the whole time. His stories always put me on the edge of my seat. He'd get me laughing a lot and he'd laugh, too. I had so much fun, I'd leave his office on a high, feeling good about myself and thinking, *This guy actually likes me!*

I didn't really know it at the time, but his story-telling was extremely helpful to me; I know it changed my life. He talked to me like I was one of his buddies, like a real person, not a scared kid. His stories helped me mature around men. By treating me like an equal, he gave me something I'd never experienced before—he broke down my wall of fear around men. Together, we were just regular guys telling tales.

One day, he'd been telling a story about something in his life that really made me laugh. That's when I admitted I didn't know much about girls or sex except what I saw in dirty movies. I was a 20-year-old virgin.

Suddenly, he sat up and wiggled his middle finger, then said . . .

Lou, you've got to play with a girl's pussy for a good while.

I see him moving his *left* middle finger. I'm dumbfounded, my eyes and mouth are wide open. I don't know how to respond. After about 20 seconds of stifling silence with Dr. Shoemaker smiling at me and smoking his cigarette, all I can think to say is . . .

But Dr. Shoemaker, I'm *right*-handed.

110

Lou, you've got to be ambidextrous.

Then he holds up and wiggles both of his middle fingers, and begins to laugh. I laugh, too. This guy is too funny. He's acting like I could be his best friend.

This was huge! This change allowed me to learn how to make friends and eventually make a living. My success started right then, sharing stories with Dr. Shoemaker like good buddies do.

CHAPTER 15
Four Hundred Dollars

"It takes a noble man to plant a seed for a tree that will some day give shade to people he may never meet."

- David Trueblood

As the summer months of 1976 go by, my dad has agreed to send me back to Ohio University. His stipulation is that it will be on a semester-to-semester basis. I have to keep my grades up to at least a "B" average. This really scares me because I never had a "B" average since I lived with my mother in California. I keep remembering that my high school GPA was 1.96 and my first year at Ohio University was barely a "C" average. But I feel more determined than ever to make it work this time. I will study twenty hours a day if I have to. There's no turning back.

Considering where I'd started with my dad four months before, it's a miracle I have gotten this far with him. All of the things Dr. Shoemaker taught me are paying off.

I'm still seeing Dr. Shoemaker twice a week during all of this time. I usually see him at five o'clock after work. If he only has a four o'clock opening, I use the excuse that I'm going to see my dermatologist, Dr. Gibson.

Although I'm getting along with my dad so much better, communication is still very trying. He has such mood swings, I never know how he will be from day to day or even hour to hour. But I must have been doing a good job because he'd even call me "Lou" at times.

He has never done this before. I need to discuss this with Dr. Shoemaker.

Dr. Shoemaker, do you think that I am "selling out" to my dad?

In what way?

Well, the fact that I do my best to get along with him, you know, sometimes I have to eat a lot of crow. He still yells at me a lot.

You're not selling out, you're growing up. Lou, let me tell you something. Your situation might get worse as the days get closer to your leaving for college.

Really?

Yes. You see, you are all that your dad has in life. He wants you beside him so you can be miserable like he is. It's absolutely killing him that he's helping you *escape* his hold on you. Does this make any sense to you?

I think so. I wonder why he's doing it then. I mean, why is he paying for school and for me to move away from him?

Because one part of him loves you and wants you to do well in life. Believe it or not, one part of him is proud of you. The other part wants you to remain by him so you can continue to be his whipping boy.

Dr. Shoemaker, can I ask you a question?

Yes.

Do you remember when you said that I had something called

an Oedipus complex?

Yes.

Well, I've been reading about that. Freud said that it is when boys fall in love with their mothers and want to kill their dads. He also said that dads fall in love with their daughters to an extent.

Yes, that's true.

Did that happen to you, too?

In a way.

How did you handle that?

I worked it out on the couch.

You did?

Yes.

Maybe that's what I need, too. Maybe I need to lie on the couch. I bet I do.

First things first, Lou.

If you could have met Sigmund Freud, would you have been afraid of him?

No, I would have invited him over for dinner.

You would?

Yes.

Wouldn't you be afraid that he would be analyzing you and your family? I mean, he invented the area that you chose to study. So isn't he *above* you?

Fuck, no. Lou, he's just a guy. You wanna hear a good one?

What?

Freud loved dope and sex.

NO WAY?

Oh, yeah, Freud was sex crazy. He thought about sex all the time.

But he was a smart guy, right?

He was a genius.

He was a genius?

No doubt about it. He was a brilliant man. The doctor who analyzed me was analyzed by a doctor who was analyzed by Freud himself.

Wow, that is so cool. So in a way I'm now linked to Freud.

Yes.

***

I find out that Dr. Shoemaker is right again. As the days grow closer to my leaving for college, my dad gets a lot worse, berating me in front of people and being in a terrible mood almost daily.

Dr. Shoemaker, he's driving me crazy. He yells at me every day. I can't take it anymore. I want to kill that mother fucker.

What should I do?

Keep talking.

I only have one more week to go, but I don't think I can make it. I'm afraid I'm going to yell back at him. If I do, he might just say "screw college." What do you think I should do?

Keep talking.

He's such an asshole. I hate him.

Lou, would you like to pray for that mother fucker? I'll pray with you if you'd like.

No, that's OK. I appreciate it, though.

What can you say, Lou? The guy is fucked up.

You know what else, Dr. Shoemaker?

What?

He's not going to give me any money to leave for school. I'm going to need money for books and gasoline.

Lou, it's his last effort to fuck with you. He's still having a hard time letting go. One part of him wants you to do well, but another part wants you to come crawling back to him with your tail between your legs.

So what can I do?

All you can do is be nice to him and hope that he'll come around.

When the day finally arrives for me to leave for college, I have a three o'clock visit with Dr. Shoemaker. This will be my last one with him for a while. Before my appointment, I pack my car to the brim and say goodbye to everyone. My dad doesn't give me enough money for incidentals and books. I'm doomed. How will I make it?

I drive out to see Dr. Shoemaker and thank him for all that he did for me. We both agree that I should keep seeing him even though I'm at college. Athens, Ohio, is only three hours away so I could sneak into town when I needed to and keep him informed of my progress.

As my visit ends, I stand up to shake his hand. Then something happens that totally floors me. Dr. Shoemaker opens the top drawer of his desk and pulls out four 100-dollar bills. He gives them to me. Unbelievable.

Good luck, Lou. You'll do just fine. Call me when you can.

Tears flood my eyes as I thank him with all my heart.

CHAPTER 16
Ohio University

"Dictionary is the only place where success comes before work. Hard work is the price we must pay for success. I think you can accomplish anything if you're willing to pay the price."

- Vince Lombardi

Driving to Athens, Ohio, I have a lot of mixed feelings. One part of me is scared to death because I'm driving three hours away from Pittsburgh and I do not know a soul in Athens. The other part of me is excited to see the Ohio University campus again.

It's been a year and a half since I'd last been there. I remember it as one of the most beautiful places I'd ever seen in my life. Located in southeast Ohio about one hour southeast of Columbus, Ohio, it has about 16,000 students on a beautiful campus surrounded by rolling hills and beautiful trees. A small river called the Hocking runs through the campus, making it the type of campus that colleges ideally look like in the movies. The small town of Athens itself is known only for being a college town.

Some famous people who attended Ohio University are Matt Lauer of TV's Today Show; Mike Schmidt, Hall of Fame baseball player; Paul Newman, actor and entrepreneur; Ed O'Neill, TV actor on Married With Children; Arsenio Hall, TV host; Richard Dean Anderson from the TV show MacGyver; and Jay Mariotti, sports columnist and TV personality.

What's helping my anxiety most during the drive to school is remembering that Dr. Shoemaker told me he's only as far away as a telephone, that I can visit him whenever I need to. I love the fact that Athens is far enough to get away from my dad yet close enough to visit Dr. Shoemaker.

One day during my first week at school, this cute girl in her second year walks up to me as I'm approaching the dorm cafeteria for lunch. She just starts talking to me. As we walk into the cafeteria, she tells me her name is Vicky* and even asks if she could sit next to me. She's treating me as though I'm a "normal" person. This really blows my mind. A girl has never done this to me in my life. Doesn't she know that I am a jerk and my dad's whipping boy?

Vicky is about five-foot-three and has brown hair. She hardly wears makeup and, to me, is a natural beauty. I find out she's in her second year at the University, doing a major in electrical engineering. That's totally unbelievable to me. I would last ten minutes with a major as difficult as engineering. My major is undecided still and my courses are pretty much the basic math, English, history, geography subjects. Vicky is taking subjects like differential equations and advanced calculus. To me, she is brilliant.

She asks me about my major. I tell her I'm working on a four-year degree in business and I want to fly for the airlines someday. She asks why I'm not in engineering. I'm truthful and say that I don't have the high school background needed to handle those subjects.

I also find out that she lives in Bellaire, Ohio, which is right along the Ohio River near Wheeling, West Virginia, and pretty much on my route when I drive back to Pittsburgh. She loves hearing that because she doesn't have a car on campus. She asks if she could hitch a ride with me the next time I drive home to Pittsburgh. I say sure, but this scares me even more. That means I'd have to drive more than two hours with her in my car each way. What would I talk about with her? Plus, I know that my dad would never approve of my actually talking to a girl, especially one that I'm interested in. He HATED it if I talked to girls. In fact, before I left for school, when he caught me

---

* Not her real name.

talking to a cute teller in the bank, he yelled at me right in the bank and embarrassed the hell out of me.

I'm only at school three weeks when my dad calls me at my dorm and yells at me. He says he received a $5 parking ticket from the Ohio University police and that he's going to stop paying for any more school for me. He shouted, "I paid for this semester and there's nothing I can do now about that, but that's all I'm going to pay for. After this semester, you're done!"

I hang up the phone crying. I have a lot of studying to do and this call makes it impossible to concentrate. I need to see Dr. Shoemaker badly, so I call him and set up an appointment for Friday at five o'clock. That means I won't have to leave campus until noon that day so at least I can attend almost all of my classes.

I tell Vicky my plan. She says she wants to go home to Bellaire and retrieve some things she needs and would love to ride with me. On the ride to her house, she tells me a number of unbelievable things. She tells me she's a very sexual person and has had sex with at least a hundred guys already. I almost have a heart attack. Here I am—a virgin! Of course she doesn't know that and I don't tell her, but if I did feel a little intimidated by her at first, *now* I'm totally petrified of her. Thank God, I'm going to see Dr. Shoemaker. I need to talk to him BADLY.

Finally, I drop Vicky off in Bellaire and continue on to Pittsburgh. Telling me about how much sex she's had scares the hell out of me. I have so much to tell Dr. Shoemaker about my dad and Vicky, and I need to hear what he has to say.

Dr. Shoemaker, thank you for making time for me.

No problem, Lou. Tell me about school.

Oh my God. My dad called me and said I got a $5 parking

ticket and that he's so angry, he isn't going to pay for any more college after this semester. What am I going to do?

Lou, let me tell you what's going on. Your dad is upset because he realizes he's losing control of you now that you are away from him. The only control he has over you is money. He misses you, Lou. It's killing him that you are cutting the cord from him. Remember, you're all he has in his miserable life. It's also killing him that he's actually helping you to cut the cord. So in a sense, he is doing the one thing he really doesn't want to do. Mostly, he's just scared of losing you, Lou.

Can I ask you something?

OK.

Weren't you afraid of losing your kids when they went away to college?

Hell no.

Why?

Because I was happy they were growing up and experiencing life.

You were *happy* about that?

Yes.

Wow.

Lou, that's *normal*. That's how most parents are.

Really?

Yes. Lou, I have my own life. I don't need my kids around me to be happy. In fact, seeing them grow up and become happy *makes* me happy.

Wow. What a difference from my dad.

I know.

So what can I do?

Lou, your dad senses that you're not grateful for what he's doing for you.

Really?

Yes. Let me ask you something. How often do you call him or write him?

I haven't done either.

You see. You need to let your dad know that you appreciate what he's doing for you. Right now, he feels like you don't appreciate the sacrifices he's made for you.

Wow.

You should call him.

But I hate talking to him.

Then write him notes. Thank him. Tell him how much you appreciate him. Believe me, he would love to hear that from you.

I can do that.

Lou, he's afraid of losing you. Let him know that you'll always be his friend. Remember, he never had a chance to go to college and leave Carnegie. When you think of it what he's doing for you, it *really* is amazing.

I think you're right. I'll write him a note every day if I have to.

Good.

Dr. Shoemaker, there's something else that's happened to me.

What's that?

I met this girl at college named Vicky. She lives in Bellaire, Ohio, and I just drove her home. You should see her; she's pretty and smart. Her major is electrical engineering.

He nods and takes a drag from his cigarette.

Lou, would you like some tea?

OK.

So you met a girl from Bellaire?

Yes. Get a load of this. She told me that she's had sex with over a hundred guys.

How old is she?

Twenty.

She's a whore.

No she's not. She's majoring in electrical engineering. She's very smart.

I don't care how smart she is; she's a whore.

What do you mean by that?

Lou, any woman who is twenty years old and has fucked over a hundred guys is a whore. She's fucked up. Whores can suck off a hundred guys in a day. It takes no talent to be a whore.

Really?

Yes.

But she seems nice. She came right up to me and said hi and was friendly to me.

I think she wanted to fuck you, Lou.

You think?

Yes.

Wow. After she told me about how many guys she's been with, I got really intimidated by her.

You'd better be careful; she might have a venereal disease.

Really?

There's a good chance.

Dr. Shoemaker, you have grown daughters. You wouldn't want them to have had sex with that many guys, would you?

If they did, I would figure that I did something wrong.

Really?

Really.

Wow. So you think Vicky is fucked up?

Yes. Lou, I walked my daughter down the aisle when she got married. I don't know this for sure but I think that she was a virgin.

Wow.

I think so.

Weren't you mad when she was getting married?

Mad?

Yeah.

Why would I be mad?

My dad would be mad if I got married.

That's because he would be losing you to a woman. He wants you all to himself. It's a sick relationship.

You didn't want your kids all to yourself?

No. I had my own life with their mother before she died. I always wanted them to find someone special, too.

Wow. I must really be fucked up.

You'll be OK. How is school?

Before my dad called me, I was doing OK. I have five classes and I study all the time. I don't even go to parties. I'm afraid of screwing up my one chance to escape my dad and I don't want to blow it. All I want to do is *graduate*.

So, I take it that no one knows you're in town right now?

That's right. If my dad knew I came into town and didn't see him, he would go crazy. After I leave here, I'm going right back to Bellaire to pick up Vicky and then back to Athens.

Keep in touch. Call me when you need to see me again. I'll make room for you.

As he walks me to the door, he hands me forty dollars.

Here, take this for gas, Lou.

Are you sure you want to give me this?

Yes. Keep your chin up.

OK. Thank you very much, Dr. Shoemaker.

CHAPTER 17
Dear Dad . . .

"At times our own light goes out and it is rekindled by a spark from another person. Each of us has a cause to think with deep gratitude of those who have lighted the flame within us."

- Dr. Albert Schweitzer

As I leave Dr. Shoemaker's office, I have so much new information to think about. At least now I understand why my dad's torturing me. Dr. Shoemaker predicted this might happen. It even happened like he said in the weeks before I left for school. I'm amazed at how smart and generous Dr. Shoemaker is.

Now he's telling me that Vicky is screwed up, too. As I drive back to Bellaire, all I can think about is what Dr. Shoemaker said—that I really need to thank my dad for what he's done so far for me. Maybe it will help if I formally thank him. It sounds good in theory, so I know what I have to do—write to my dad and thank him for helping me.

I pick up Vicky at her house and she invites me in. She lives with her mother who is quite old. I think she told me her dad died when she was a young girl. On the way back to Athens, I find it hard to keep a conversation going.

Although I'd drive her to Bellaire on a few more occasions, I believe she knew I was a waste of time for her. I just had too much to worry about with my dad and graduating to get involved with a girl. How could I possibly get close to a girl when my dad is calling me every day and threatening to take me out of school? I just keep hoping that

Dr. Shoemaker's prediction that "your day will come" will be true. All I know for sure is that I'm in no condition to get close to anyone. I'm on a mission to graduate from Ohio University and get on with the airlines. That's my prize. If I can do that, I'll be free of my dad and can live a happy life. Nothing will stop me. Nothing.

As soon as I get back to my dorm room, I write my dad this letter.

> Dear Dad,
> I just want to thank you for all that you are doing and all that you have done for me. I could never do any of this without you. I know that you never had a dad to help you like you're helping me. All I know is this: Someday, when I'm flying with the airlines all over the world, I'll be sure to tell all the other pilots that I couldn't have done anything without the help of my dad.
> Love,
> Lou

***

At least three times a week the whole time I was at college, I sent my dad a letter similar to this one. Guess what? It worked! Dr. Shoemaker was right again. My dad *loved* those letters. And you know what? The more letters I wrote, the more I really felt the truth of the words. I know my dad really was doing something that was painful for him to do by going against his own script to keep me near him. Paying for my college and paying for me to live three hours away from him was like having to cut the cord himself. I really needed to give him credit. I started to appreciate my dad a lot more.

From this point on, my relationship with my dad began to change forever. I finally got it. I kept doing my best to edify him. And my dad began to respect me a lot more. He stopped fighting me. I think he actually started *liking* me. And I began thinking, "The poor guy hates himself so much, maybe I can brighten up his life a little."

The good grades on my first semester report card was a start. I got—

Algebra	A
English	A
Geography	A-
Psychology	B+
Shop	D+

To get a two-year degree in aviation technology, I had to take shop, even though I wasn't any good at it. In this class, I had to take apart a lawn mower engine and put it back together—and get the engine to start! But mine didn't start. Somehow I knew that it wouldn't. I'm the most unmechanical person in the world.

Still, I made the dean's list with this report card. My dad did make a big fuss over that D+ but I think he was actually surprised by my good grades.

* * *

One day while I'm in the cafeteria, I overhear a guy tell his friend that Vicky would come over to his room and give him a quick "blow job" between classes. This really freaks me out and even depresses me. I keep thinking, "What's wrong with *me*? She liked *me* before she met that other guy. He even has long hair in a ponytail. He looks like a hippie."

I can't wait to see Dr. Shoemaker again. I want to bring him my report card and tell him about Vicky.

Dr. Shoemaker, here are my grades.

He looks at the printout.

Lou, you did great. You should be very proud of yourself.

My dad went nuts over that D+ in shop class.

Don't worry about him, Lou. He's just blowing off steam. I think he now realizes that you're going to make it and it scares him. He'll be OK. I think you did a fantastic job, especially considering what you had to deal with from him.

Dr. Shoemaker, I wrote those letters like you told me and they worked great. My dad seems to respect me more. He's already paid for the next semester.

That's great. Would you like some tea, Lou?

OK.

Dr. Shoemaker pours us some tea and then he sits back in his swivel chair to enjoy smoking his cigarette.

Dr. Shoemaker, wait until you hear this.

I'm all ears.

I was sitting in the cafeteria last week and I overheard this guy tell his friend that Vicky comes over to his dorm room almost every day and gives him a "blow job."

So, what's wrong with that?

There's *nothing* wrong with that?

No.

Really?

Really.

Wow, this is unbelievable to hear.

She just wanted some lunch.

She WHAT??

I stare at him with my mouth hanging open. He laughs out loud before saying it again.

Yeah, she wanted some lunch, Lou. I guess she was hungry, right?

I'm blown away by this. I stare at him speechless.

Lou, it's no big deal. They are both consenting adults, right?

I guess. All I do is study all the time.

Lou, I think it's good that you study, but on weekends, you should get your dick sucked if you want to.

I actually fall out of my chair onto his floor. Then I get right back up. Dr. Shoemaker laughs out loud again.

You're CRAZY.

I know, Lou. I've been told that before.

Is this how all psychiatrists talk?

I have no idea how other psychiatrists talk, Lou. Most of them are fucked up anyway.

You're unbelievable.

He just smiles at me.

Lou, our time is about up. I'm real proud of you. Keep studying but please have some fun too, OK?

He walks me to the door and shakes my hand.

Keep in touch, Lou.

Don't worry, I will.

CHAPTER 18
My First Time

"With everything that has happened to you, you can either feel sorry for yourself or treat what has happened as a gift. Everything is either an opportunity to grow or an obstacle to keep you from growing. You get to choose."

- Unknown

Even though Dr. Shoemaker wanted me to have fun at college, I felt too afraid. All I did was go to my classes and study, even on weekends.

The next semester, my grades were all As and Bs. My dad hadn't been bothering me anymore and that's a relief. But he began pressuring me to work with him during the summer break. This absolutely freaked me out. No way can I subject myself to him for a complete summer!

So I came up with a plan. About two months before summer break, I sent out resumes to flight schools in Ohio and Michigan. I gave my return address as my dorm room at True House on campus. I didn't want my dad to get wind of my plan.

I received a few offers, then took a small plane from the Ohio University airport and checked out two of them. On the first trip, I went up to Detroit and on the second over to Cincinnati. I checked out both offers and decided to pick the one at the Clermont County Airport near Cincinnati.

As I flew to these places to check them out, I actually got the courage to ask two attractive coeds if they'd like to take an airplane ride with me. These were separate trips, of course. Both girls seemed excited to go. On the way back from the first trip in Detroit, I actually spent the night with one of them in my dorm room. This is my first experience with a girl. I was scared to death. All I could think of was telling Dr. Shoemaker about it.

***

The following weekend, I'm back in his office.

Dr. Shoemaker, you're not going to believe what happened to me.

What?

I actually spent the night with a girl and she was beautiful.

How did it go?

Not too well.

Why?

Well, she began kissing me all over and then she started to give me oral sex as I was lying on my bed.

He nods.

Well, I couldn't have an orgasm.

Were you erect?

Pretty much, I guess.

What do you think was the matter?

Well, she kept sucking on me and I was thinking that if I have an orgasm, she'll get mad at me.

She'll get mad at you?

Yeah.

Why would she get mad at you?

Well, I didn't want to have an orgasm while she was sucking on me because that's gross, isn't it?

Lou, some girls like that.

You're kidding?

No, I'm not kidding.

Now that you say that, I told her that I was afraid to come because it might get messy. Guess what she said to me?

What?

She said that it would have been OK and that she would have "gotten into it." Can you believe that?

Yes, I believe that. Lou, some girls even *swallow* it.

WHAT!

Some girls love that. They'll swallow it.

You've got to be kidding me.

No, I'm not. Didn't you say that she wished you had come and that she would have gotten into it?

Yes.

Well, there you go. I'm not making this up, Lou. You've got to get into the game eventually. One thing at a time. You're making progress.

You really think so?

Yes. Tell me, Lou, overall how did you feel when you were with her?

Scared.

Do you know why?

No.

Lou, you were scared because you were afraid that your dad would catch you.

I was?

Yes.

How do I get over that?

Keep talking.

Just keep talking?

Yes, keep talking.

My dad wants me to work with him making rubber stamps this summer, but there's no way I can go back to that now. So I found a summer job in Cincinnati teaching people to fly and flying charters.

Have you told your dad yet?

No, not yet. Get a load of this. He actually drove to Athens to visit me last week.

Really?

Yes. He said that he had some business to attend to there, but I know he was lying. He has no business in Athens, Ohio.

How did the visit go?

Actually, it went great. He took me out to dinner and then breakfast the next morning. He even gave me $100 to help me out.

That's great.

Except he wouldn't visit my dorm. I begged him to see where I lived, but he wouldn't do it.

Do you know why, Lou?

No.

It's because he was intimidated by the school and the students.

You really think so?

Yes. Remember, he has never gotten out of Carnegie. Deep down, he's still about ten years old inside.

Hearing you say that about my dad makes me feel sad for him.

It is sad, Lou, but you can see that your dad seems to be a lot nicer to you now.

It's a miracle, Dr. Shoemaker. It's really a miracle. It would *not* have happened without you. Please be careful. I don't want anything to happen to you. I still need you.

I'm not going anywhere, Lou. You know where to reach me.

CHAPTER 19
"You Write It"

"Any time you have a chance to help someone and you don't, you're wasting your time on earth."

- Roberto Clemente

My head was again spinning from all of the information I was learning from Dr. Shoemaker. All I could think of was my dad being afraid to step on a college campus to see where I lived. He stayed at the Ohio University Inn in Athens the whole time. The guy who had always intimidated me so much was *actually afraid to visit me at school*. This blew my mind.

My dad seemed proud of me because, the semester before, I got a job at the University airport as a flight instructor to incoming freshmen. So in a sense, I was on the school payroll. My dad loved that. I was actually making money—not much, but at least something.

With the summer of 1977 getting closer, I had to tell my dad about my plans to live in Cincinnati and teach flying to build up my flight time and experience. Of course, he yelled at me and threw a fit, but he came around. He resigned himself to the fact that taking this job made sense.

Working in Cincinnati that summer—the summer that Elvis died—did wonders for my relationship with my dad. He was growing to respect me more and more. Sometimes, he would call the flight school to say hi to me. One time, he was told I was in Tennessee flying a charter. He was so impressed, he even walked down his street to tell Reba and Harold how well I was doing. That's unbelievable considering where our relationship had been only two years before.

Still, during all those years I attended college, I made sure that I stayed busy and never had to come home to Carnegie again, even for school breaks or holidays. If I did, I knew he'd yell at me. Besides, being away from home taught me that I could do things for myself and really boosted my confidence.

**

Back at school in September, I add up all of my credits and I'm only a few short of being a senior. (I'd received credit by exam for a few semesters because of all my flying experience.) I also find out that if I can get a Boeing 727 flight engineer rating, I can get another semester's worth of credit for that. I learn that a flight school in Atlanta offers that course around Christmas break. In this five-week course, I'd learn about hydraulics, fuel, and pneumatics on a Boeing 727 jet. The school costs $10,000. Getting my license (or rating) would greatly enhance my resume for work with the airlines. Somehow I'm able to convince my dad to pay for it.

I pass the test. Getting that rating allows me to graduate from Ohio University in March of 1978 instead of June. I'm now a college graduate! Unbelievable. My dad and grandparents are so proud of me. In the history of the Panesi family, I'm the first one to ever graduate from college.

During my next visit with Dr. Shoemaker, I feel ecstatic.

> Dr. Shoemaker, I did it! Can you believe that I am now a college graduate? It was only three years ago that I was homeless. Look at what you've done for me!

> Lou, *you* did it. I'm very proud of you.

> Dr. Shoemaker, can I ask you a question?

Sure.

Why don't you write a book about what you did for me? I really think that it would sell.

Lou, I really don't have a desire to write a book at this time in my life.

You don't?

Not at all. I'll tell you what—*you* write it.

Me?

Yes, you.

You want me to write a book?

I think that you could do it.

You really think that?

Yes, I do. I think it could help a lot of people.

We'll see, Dr. Shoemaker. I've got a lot to accomplish before I can ever do something like that. I still need to get on with the airlines. I'm going to send out resumes to all of the smaller commuter airlines so I can build up my flight time. I've only got 800 hours and the major airlines want at least 2,000 hours of experience. In the meantime, I have a job as a flight instructor at the Butler County airport just north of Pittsburgh.

Our time is up, Lou. Can you come back next week?

Yes. I'll see you then.

As I drive away from Dr. Shoemaker's office, all I can think about is his suggestion. *Is he serious about me writing a book?*

CHAPTER 20
"What's Wrong With Me?"

"Life begins as a quest of the child to discover the man and ends as a journey by the man to rediscover the child."

- Laurens Van Der Post

While flight instructing at Butler Airport after college, I wasn't at all happy anymore. I still had a lot of anxiety. I still bit my fingernails and my back still bled. However, I was able to be a good instructor to my students. In fact, about 15 years later, a student I had at this time became a captain for US Airways and we bumped into each other. He gave me a great compliment. He told me I was the best instructor that he'd ever had.

I only worked as a flight instructor for six months before my big break—I got hired as a co-pilot of a turbo prop plane at Allegheny County Airport flying executives all around the east coast. It only paid $600 a month, but it allowed me to build up valuable flight experience that the airlines require.

***

About this time, I realize I have a severe problem. I'm deathly afraid of authority figures. This includes the captains I fly with. They want to be friendly with me, but I can't be friendly in return. I look at them as extensions of my dad, I guess.

Dr. Shoemaker, what is *wrong* with me? I'm scared to death of the people I work around. Everyone else seems to be fitting in except me. There is something *very* wrong with me.

Lou, you think that these people are your dad; they're not. Your dad's treatment of you as a young teen is fucking up your relationships with authority figures. Your dad and grandfather tortured you for years. The fact that you were loved as an infant and little boy saved your life.[1] The love you received early in life gave you a basis for healing. If you didn't have that, I don't think I could ever help you.

Can I be fixed?

I think so, but it takes time.

I think I need to lie on the couch. I've had enough of this face-to-face stuff. It's not working anymore.

Lou, doing psychoanalysis takes a lot of effort. You have to commit to it five days a week.

Really?

Yes.

I can't do that while I'm working because I go out of town on trips, plus I have to be on call when I'm home.

Lou, lying on the couch is not a be-all and end-all. In fact, you might get worse before you get better.

You're kidding, right?

No, I'm not. It's not easy lying on the couch.

So that won't fix me right away?

[1] Dr. Shoemaker made this assessment after previously seeing photos of me from infancy to five years old.

I don't think so. It's a tough process. I don't think the time is right yet for you.

I only worked a few months at Allegheny County Airport when a commuter Airline out of Harrisburg, Pennsylvania, gave me a job as a co-pilot on a turbo prop plane. I was flying people all over the state—most of the flights hopped from small airports to major ones like Pittsburgh and Philadelphia.

For this job, I was based in Johnstown, Pennsylvania. There, I got an apartment by myself. It gave me a fixed schedule so I could see Dr. Shoemaker regularly.

***

Now it seems like on every visit, I tell Dr. Shoemaker that I need to be on the couch. I don't really even know what the couch can do for me—except I still have a gut feeling this face-to-face style isn't helping me anymore.

I still have my same problems with authority-figure men. In fact, it's worse; I'm petrified of *everyone*. I'm suffering so much, I don't know how long I can keep working at this job.

On my next visit to Dr. Shoemaker, I tell him about my fear of everyone.

> Dr. Shoemaker, where I live in Johnstown, a beautiful girl lives above me. I'm too afraid to talk to her but, get this. Every night, I hear her and her boyfriend having sex. This really freaks me out. What do *you* think about that?
>
> What's there to think about, Lou? It's a natural act, right?
>
> That's how you think?
>
> Of course. They're just in heat.

So it's no big deal to you?

Not at all. First, it's none of my business; second, she's just
behaving normally.

Normal? Man, I must really be *fucked up*.

Lou, your time will come.

About a month after that, I meet a girl in my apartment complex. I
have to talk to Dr. Shoemaker about my experience with her right
away.

> Dr. Shoemaker, I met this cute girl and within an hour, I was
> in bed with her, but I couldn't perform. **What is wrong with
> me?**

I begin crying.

> Lou, tell me the whole story.

> I met her in the laundry room and we began talking. She
> invited me up to her apartment and, before long, we were
> kissing on her couch.

> Tell me more about that.

> Well, she was lying on the couch and I was kneeling on the
> floor kissing her.

> Why were you kneeling on the floor? Were you *praying* to
> her?

> What do you mean?

> I mean, why weren't you *on the couch* with her? You're acting
> like she's the Virgin Mary by kneeling on the floor.

Really?

Yes. Lou, you've got to get with the program. That kneeling is terrible body language on your part. But tell me more.

Well, we kissed for a while, then I got up to close her drapes.

Why did you do that?

I was afraid someone might see us.

Then what did you do?

Then we went into her bedroom. I closed the bedroom door and locked it. After that, I couldn't get hard. Dr. Shoemaker, what the *fuck* is the matter with me?

I cry harder.

Lou, you're afraid that your dad is going to catch you. That's why you had to close the blinds and lock her bedroom door. You can't seem to get him out of your head.

I'm doomed. Is there any hope for me?

Yes, I believe so.

What do I have to do to get over this *shit*?

Keep talking.

***

By October of 1979, I couldn't take it anymore. I was falling apart, barely functioning. I could still fly a plane, but I felt so depressed, I had to leave my job.

It's funny, but my dad thought I was still working so he began fun-neling money to me to help him with his taxes. I ended up moving to Penn Hills, on the east side of Pittsburgh far from my dad's house. He had no idea that I'd left my job or he would have pounced all over that. The money he was giving me, though, saved me. It allowed me to get an apartment and buy food while I worked on my prob-lems with Dr. Shoemaker.

***

One day about this time, I enter his office to take my normal place in my chair in front of his desk. As I do, he grabs my shirt sleeve and nudges me over to the couch.

I can't believe it. I'm now going to start doing psychoanalysis! I have no idea what I'm in for; I just know that something big will happen. Little did I know how big . . .

CHAPTER 21
"I Hate You"

*"What the heart gives away is never lost because it stays
in the hearts of others."*

- David Lam

Finally I'm lying on the couch. Dr. Shoemaker sits in a big soft chair behind my head for the first time. I can't see him.

What do I say, Dr. Shoemaker?

Say whatever comes to your mind.

What do you mean by that?

Just say whatever you want to say, Lou.

I don't know what you mean. I don't want to say the wrong thing.

You *can't* say the wrong thing. Just say whatever you want to say.

But I'm afraid to do that.

Why?

Because I'll most likely say something that isn't appropriate and you'll get mad at me.

Everything you say is appropriate, Lou.

I'm scared.

Scared of what?

I'm scared that you will yell at me.

Why would I yell at you?

Because I'll say the wrong things and you'll feel like I'm wasting your time and then you'll get mad at me.

He doesn't respond.

Please give me an idea what to talk about.

He doesn't respond.

I don't want to talk if I don't know what the ground rules are.

There are no ground rules, Lou. You need to talk about ninety percent of the time. I'm just here to help you along.

But what if I get off on a tangent that you don't like?

No response.

I already know what's going to happen.

No response.

You're going to criticize me for talking about the wrong stuff and wasting your time.

No response.

Now I've asked you very nicely to help me with the ground rules so that I don't waste your valuable time. But you won't help me understand how this is supposed to work.

No response.

Why won't you help me?

He talks in a very soft voice . . .

Just say whatever comes to your mind, Lou.

I already know exactly what is going to happen here.

No response.

Here's what will happen. I'm going to do as you say and start talking about whatever comes to my mind and you're going to yell at me and say, "Don't talk about THAT STUFF; talk about THIS STUFF." Let me tell you something, IF YOU DO THAT, I'M GOING TO GET OFF OF THIS FUCKING COUCH AND COME BACK THERE AND PUNCH YOU RIGHT IN THE MOUTH. WHAT DO YOU THINK ABOUT THAT?

No response.

I KNOW ABOUT PEOPLE LIKE YOU. DEEP DOWN, YOU'RE A PIECE OF SHIT. GO AHEAD, SAY SOMETHING TO ME LIKE THAT. I DARE YOU. IF YOU DO, YOU MOTHER FUCKER, I'LL GRAB YOU BY THE FUCKING NECK AND THROW YOU OUT THE FUCKING WINDOW. YOU FAT MOTHER FUCKER. I HATE YOU, YOU PIECE OF SHIT. WHAT DO YOU THINK ABOUT THAT, YOU

MOTHER FUCKER?

Before I know it, Dr. Shoemaker interrupts my tirade. My forty-five minutes are up.

I'll see you tomorrow at nine-thirty in the morning.

Dr. Shoemaker's words break me out of my trancelike state.

What?

I'll see you tomorrow at nine-thirty.

It takes me a minute to get out my trance. I need to sit up and put my feet on the floor. Finally, I turn to Dr. Shoemaker. He's getting up from his chair as though nothing happened at all.

Dr. Shoemaker, I'm so sorry I said those things to you.

I'll see you tomorrow, Lou.

I show myself to the door and let myself out. What just happened in there?

CHAPTER 22
Transference

"Happiness is the interval between periods of unhappiness."

- Don Marquis

I left Dr. Shoemaker's office in a daze. Lying on the couch seemed like I was being hypnotized. All I thought about on my drive home was this: "How *could* I talk to Dr. Shoemaker that way? Here's a guy who's seeing me for *nothing*. I know that he cares about me, yet I end up calling him names like that. I must be an evil person."

The thing I remembered most about that whole visit was finally getting off the couch to leave his office. I looked over at him to apologize for the terrible things I'd said. But he didn't seem upset at all. No big deal to him. "Lou, I'll see you tomorrow" was all he said.

***

The day after I swore at him, I arrive at Dr. Shoemaker's office. He gently opens his door and lets me in. I walk to the couch and lie down. Dr. Shoemaker takes his place in his oversized, comfortable cloth chair behind me.

> Dr. Shoemaker, I want to apologize to you for the things I said to you yesterday.

> Lou, what you said is perfectly normal.

> *It is?*

Yes.

Why?

It's called transference. You were talking to me the way you always wanted to talk to your dad but couldn't.

So, it didn't surprise you?

No, I expected it.

You did?

Yes.

Is this something that Freud invented?

Yes.

I just hope you remember that if I yell at you, it's because of this transference and not because I really hate you.

No response.

I mean, I don't want you to dump me over this. You won't dump me, will you?

No, I won't dump you.

I just lie there for a few minutes without saying anything. Finally, Dr. Shoemaker breaks the silence.

What are you thinking, Lou?

I was thinking about this dream I had last night.

Tell me about it.

I was walking down the street with Roberto Clemente and we were arm in arm like best friends. What do you think that means?

What do *you* think that it means?

I don't know.

Think about it. See what you can come up with.

We're both silent for a minute or two while I try to figure out what that dream means.

I don't know. Do *you* know?

Yes, I know.

What does it mean?

Lou, it is a "wish" dream. You wished that you could have been friends with Roberto Clemente. In a sense, it's a healthy dream.

I start crying.

I miss him so much. I can't believe that he's dead. He was my whole life as a kid. I loved him so much.

He was a great ball player, Lou. And a good role model for you.

My dad hated him so much. He called him a nigger in front of me all the time.

I cry harder.

> Lou, your dad was jealous. He hated that you liked Clemente
> more than him.

> How could I *not*? Look at the difference between the two.
> Clemente even died trying to help other people. My dad
> hates everyone. I can't believe he is dead.[2] The time has gone
> by so fast. It seems like yesterday that I was going to Forbes
> Field to watch him play.

> His type comes around once every hundred years, Lou.

I cry harder.

> That MOTHER FUCKER. How could my dad have said those
> things about him. I HATE THAT MOTHER FUCKER SO
> MUCH.

No response. He lets me vent. I don't say anything for about two
minutes. Finally, Dr. Shoemaker asks me a question in a low voice.

> Lou, what are you thinking about?

> I'm thinking about how frightened I am of everyone. When I
> left here yesterday, my stomach was in knots. I didn't want to
> see anyone. All I could do was go back to my apartment and
> go to bed.

> Lou, I'm going to write you a prescription for some medica-
> tion. It will help you with your anxiety.

> Dr. Shoemaker, I had another dream last night.

---

[2] Clemente died on December 31, 1972, in a plane crash while en route to deliver aid
to earthquake victims in Nicaragua.

Tell me about it.

I was a pilot at the airport and I witnessed first-hand a plane crashing on takeoff. It was a four-engine propeller plane and it tried to take off with only two engines being started. Of course, it couldn't get airborne. I saw it crash into the terminal and kill a lot of people. What do you think that dream means?

What do *you* think it means?

I don't know.

I want you to think about it, Lou.

Do you know what it means?

Yes, but I want you to try and figure it out.

Why?

I want you to be able to analyze your own dreams.

Do you think that I can learn that?

Yes. Think about that dream and we'll discuss it tomorrow.

OK.

CHAPTER 23
The Anger Comes Out

*"Anger is a killing thing: it kills the man who angers,
for each rage leaves him less than he had been
before-it takes something from him."*

- Louis L'Armour

I had gone home that morning trying to figure out what my dream meant and couldn't. I felt hopeless analyzing dreams. It seemed way too complicated. So I went to bed and tried to sleep. Lying on the couch was draining. Little did I know that it would get much worse. During that time, my visits there took place every day, five days a week, for the next three-and-a-half years.

Typically on these visits, Dr. Shoemaker would open his door, take off his glasses, and hold them in his right hand while making eye contact with me in the waiting room. Then he'd gently motion for me to come in and take my place on his couch. As time went by, it became increasingly hard for me to make eye contact with him; the transference had made me hate him so much. That's *all* I could think about—hating this man.

***

The next day, I'm lying on the couch. Right away, I tell Dr. Shoemaker that I'd been thinking about my dream of the airplane trying to take off on only two engines.

I have no idea what this dream means.

Lou, it means that you don't feel that you are capable right now of flying yourself. *You* are the airplane trying to get airborne with only half of your engines working. It's symbolic of the state you're in.

Do you *really* think that's what my dream means?

Yes. Can you see the correlation?

I think so.

I had another dream last night.

What did you dream?

Do you know the actor who plays in horror movies by the name of Vincent Price?

Yes.

Well, I was in a big fight with him. We were fighting to the death. He was trying his best to kill me. Finally, I got the better of him. I had him pinned down and was sitting on his chest. I had this big knife and was holding it above his head as though I was going to kill him. He begged me not to kill him. I had to think for a minute about whether I wanted to do it. Finally, I said FUCK IT and then I turned my head away as I drove the knife into his head and killed him. Do you think that dream means anything?

Yes.

What?

I want you to think about it.

Minutes go by and I still have no idea what this Vincent Price dream could mean.

I have no idea.

Vincent Price is your dad. You are fighting and killing your dad. It just shows how much hatred you harbor toward him.

Really? That's nothing. I hate that mother fucker so bad—do you know what I keep thinking about?

What?

I think about tying him up on a table naked. Then I would like to take razor blades and slice him up into little pieces and then I would like to pour vinegar all over him. Then I would like to get hedge clippers and cut off his dick and then get a sledge hammer and BASH THAT FUCKER'S HEAD IN. What do you think about THAT?

Keep talking.

And then there's my fucking mother. That bitch sent me back to him when I was in 5th grade to get tortured. I hate her, too. Do you know what I'd like to do to that CUNT?

No response.

Let me tell you what I would like to do to that CUNT. I'd like to get a stick of dynamite and PUT IT IN HER PUSSY AND BLOW THAT FUCKER UP. I HATE HER SO BAD. What do you think about THAT?

Keep talking, Lou.

I hate both of those FUCKERS. They ruined my whole childhood. When other kids my age were talking to girls, my dad was calling me a bum and a jerk every morning at the break-fast table before school. It's no wonder I'd skip school. I'd drive my car to the mall and sleep in it all day. I was too ashamed of myself to face people. Don't you agree that what he did to me was terrible?

Yes.

YOU'RE just as bad. I hate you, too. All of you people my dad's age are MOTHER FUCKERS. You're all alike. I bet you would have done the same thing to me that my dad did. What do you think about that, you FUCKING ASSHOLE?

I'm not your dad.

I DON'T GIVE A FUCK. YOU'RE ALL THE SAME. FUCK YOU.
SOMEONE NEEDS TO DIE FOR DOING THIS TO ME.

That's the fucking Italian in you coming out.

What?

Italians want revenge on people who fuck them. That's the dago in you coming out, Lou.

Aren't you afraid of me?

Fuck no. I'm not afraid of you or your dad.

***

As the years went by, this was all I did. I yelled and screamed and cried about every little thing that ever happened to me. My stomach felt like someone was cutting my guts out. The years 1979 to 1983 were pure hell for me—every day the same thing, lying on the couch, getting my anger out, and crying.

***

In 1981, something significant happens. My dad is diagnosed with colon cancer and his doctor tells the family he only has one year to live. I go and tell Dr. Shoemaker the good news.

Dr. Shoemaker, guess what?

What?

My dad has colon cancer and he should be dead *in one year*! Once he dies, you watch. I'll be happy then. I won't have him on earth to bother me anymore.

It might not be that simple, Lou.

What do you mean? Once he's gone, I'll be fine. I won't have anyone to bother me anymore. You watch. I'll have girl-friends and everything.

We'll see, Lou. I hope you're right. But don't be too surprised if you still have struggles.

Struggles? What struggles? I'll be free then. Don't you see?

I hope you're right.

You know what else?

What?

I should inherit a lot of money and I'll be able to pay you what I owe you. Do you even know how much I owe?

Yes. I've kept track.

You have?

Yes.

Wow, I bet that I owe you a lot of money. Dr. Shoemaker, let me tell you this: paying you back will be my highest priority. I hope that you know I'll pay you.

Lou, you could never truly repay me for what I've done for you.

Yes, I could. You watch. I'll do it.

You don't get my point, but that's OK.

I bet that I'll inherit about $300,000 and then I'll pay you.

Lou, the only thing I would say to you is this: If you *did* inherit that much money and you *didn't* pay me, I would stop seeing you.

Dr. Shoemaker, don't worry. That would never happen. My word is good, especially when it comes to you.

Lou, the way to truly pay me is *to pass it on.*

I actually can't believe that he'd said he would stop seeing me, but I do believe he means it. He's not a wimp. When he says he'd dump me if I didn't pay him if I came into a lot of money, I believe him. I definitely don't want Dr. Shoemaker dumping me. The idea scares the hell out of me. I still have a lot of work to do with him.

CHAPTER 24
My Back Clears Up

"To carry a grudge is like being stung to death by one bee."
- William H. Walton

All of the hatred I felt toward my dad actually confuses me. One part of me really does appreciate all of the good things he's done for me. The only problem is, whenever I lie on the couch, tons of repressed anger comes flowing out, as it does on this day.

Dr. Shoemaker, one part of me feels bad that I hate my dad so much. I mean, he *did* pay for all of my education and all of my flying. He *did* do a lot of good for me.

Yes he did, but you've had intense anger that's been built up over the years. That anger has tremendously hampered your relationships with other people. I wish that I could give you a pill to cure you, but this is the only way I know how to help you, Lou.

I have some good news. I didn't say anything to you about this earlier because I wanted to wait to see if it was a passing thing, but my back has not bled in over three months. In fact, it actually looks good now.

I get off of the couch and lift up my shirt for him to see.

It's a miracle, Dr. Shoemaker. *You* did it!

No, *you* did it, Lou. I've just been a helping hand in your progress.

I think you are a genius. Do you think that Freud could have done what you did for me?

Yes, I think so.

I want to let you know that my dad is getting worse. He has lost a lot of weight. I don't think he'll live much longer.

No response.

Guess what he said to me the other day?

What?

He told me that Roberto Clemente was a good guy.

No response.

Can you believe that?

I believe it.

***

On March 27, 1982, my dad died. His second wife Ereka had called me the day before and told me I needed to come over—he was fading fast.

When I arrived, he was lying on his bed with his eyes closed as if in a coma. I sat on the bed next to him and began telling him how much I appreciated all he'd done for me over the years. He briefly opened his eyes and looked at me with his gaunt face, then said, "I guess this is it, old buddy." I started crying and I told him that I loved him. It was the only time in my life that I'd ever said those words to him. And when I said it, I meant it.

My dad was mean to me for many years but he more than made up for it in his last six years. At age 59, he died a young man—only eight years older than I am now as I write this.

***

During that time, I actually had a girlfriend named Bea. She lived in my apartment complex and we met at a July 4th pool party there. I was glad she was 20 years older than me because I still felt scared to date women my own age. She really loved me and I loved her, too. We even had sex! When I told this to Dr. Shoemaker, he took it in stride and actually seemed happy for me.

***

In one of our sessions, I am eager to discuss something Bea asked me.

Dr. Shoemaker, I have a question that comes from Bea.

What is it?

She wants to know why I always want to bite her.

What do you mean when you say "bite her"?

Well, I bite her hand, her arm, her leg. I'm just kidding and playful. But sometimes she gets mad at me because I bite her too hard. So she wanted me to ask you why I always want to bite her. Why do you think I do that?

I think you're hungry for love, Lou.

***

Because my dad died, I inherited enough money to pay Dr. Shoemaker the $100,000 I owed him. After I paid him in full, I still had money left over, but I was immature with it. I traveled to Hawaii and took friends with me. I went out to dinner every night. I bought Armani and Ermenegildo Zegna suits. I guess I wanted to be totally opposite of my dad who never spent a dime on clothing.

One of my happiest days, though, was keeping my word and paying Dr. Shoemaker. He had earned every penny of that money. Besides, he never knew when he decided to see me for free that my dad would die young and I would inherit any money. He did it because he wanted to.

To this very day, I don't know why Dr. Shoemaker took me on as his special project.

CHAPTER 25
Dr. Shoemaker Says Goodbye

"The hardest part of anything is the beginning, and the second hardest part is letting go when it's the end."

- E. Fritz

After my dad's death, I continue to lie on the couch every day for the next year. Now, in April 1983, it seems I have a new challenge. Even before his death, I believed that I'd instantly become better, that I would be set free and live happily ever after. But I begin to realize it doesn't happen that way. I still feel afraid to grow up. Even though I have money, a fine car, a beautiful apartment, a girlfriend, and nice clothes, something still upsets me. I continue to see Dr. Shoemaker.

Dr. Shoemaker, I can't get better.

Why?

I'm afraid to.

What are you afraid of?

I don't know.

No response.

I'll give you an analogy, though.

No response.

It's as though I was sent to prison on February 2, 1966, when my mom sent me back to live with my dad. I kept telling the judge that he was putting the wrong person in jail and that I didn't do anything wrong. I was innocent. Well, the judge sentenced me anyway for a crime I didn't commit. I've been furious all these years sitting in my prison cell. And now it's 17 years later, and the warden comes into my cell and tells me that I was right after all. I *was* innocent and they *did* put me in jail by mistake. He tells me they are very sorry and I'm now free to leave my cell. You know what I said to the warden?

What?

I told the warden to go FUCK HIMSELF. I screamed, "I TOLD YOU FUCKERS THAT I WAS INNOCENT BUT YOU DIDN'T BELIEVE ME. YOU CAN *ALL* GO FUCK YOUR-SELF."

So in a sense, Lou, you're cutting your nose to spite your face?

THAT'S RIGHT. FUCK YOU, TOO. YOU'RE JUST LIKE ALL THE REST. IT'S PEOPLE LIKE YOU WHO PUT ME IN PRISON. YOU WOULDN'T LISTEN TO ME. I TOLD YOU I WAS INNOCENT.

I'm not your dad, Lou.

FUCK YOU. YOU'RE JUST AS BAD. You see, all of the other kids in 5th grade got to live their lives and be happy while I was sent off to this prison. They got to meet and talk to girls. I missed all that. I never developed. Now look at me. I'm 27 years old, but deep down I'm still living in 1966 when I was 10 years old. I never had a chance to develop.

But *now* you're free.

Yes, but I'm too scared to *try and live*. All I've known is my prison cell. The warden said he'd leave the door open for me, but I'm not leaving! I refuse to leave! I don't know any other way to live. This cell has been my home for so long now. How do I get out?

Keep talking.

"I know why the caged bird sings."
- Maya Angelou

***

The next day, I'm again in Dr. Shoemaker's office lying on the couch.

I met this young, beautiful girl yesterday but I was afraid to say anything to her.

Why?

Because my dad would get mad at me if he caught me talking to a young girl.

Dr. Shoemaker responds in a soft voice.

Lou, your dad is *dead*.

When I hear him say those words, a rage comes over me—one that I'd never experienced before. I clench my fists and start to beat myself in the face over and over again. Like a rocket, Dr. Shoemaker jumps out of his chair and grabs me, pulling me off of the couch. He goes as fast as he can, but the damage has already been done. I have two black eyes, a bloody nose, and a cut lip. I hit myself as hard as I could about ten times.

Dr. Shoemaker immediately sits me in the chair in front of his desk. He grabs a towel and goes out to get cold water and ice. There's blood all over my face and shirt.

Lou, hold this towel up to your face.

I do as he says.

What just happened?

You tell *me*, Lou.

I don't know.

Think about it.

I nod. I'm curious.

Have you ever seen anyone do that before?

Not in my office. I've seen people do it in a hospital.

Why do you think I did that?

I want *you* to try and figure out why, Lou.

Do *you* know why I did it?

Yes, but I want you to figure it out. Lou, as soon as you get home, put some ice in a towel and hold it up to your face. It will help with the swelling. I want you to think about why you did this and we'll talk about it tomorrow.

I go home and look in the mirror. I have two black eyes and a puffed-up lip. I can't think of what could have made me do such a drastic thing. But I'm sure Dr. Shoemaker will know.

***

As I walk into Dr. Shoemaker's office the next day, he motions me to sit in the chair in front of his desk.

> Look at my face, Dr. Shoemaker. It looks pretty bad. Why do you think I did that?

> Why do *you* think you did it, Lou?

> I thought about it all night and I couldn't figure out why.

> You beat yourself up because you were trying to *beat your dad out of your head.*

> I was?

> Yes.

> What do you mean?

> You had said that you couldn't talk to that young girl because your dad would get mad at you.

I nod.

> I then reminded you that your dad has been dead for over a year.

I nod.

> Lou, even though your dad is physically dead, *he is still living in your mind.* You can't seem to get rid of him. When

175

you beat yourself in the head, you were trying to beat him *out* of your head. Does that make any sense to you?

Yes.

No response. Dr. Shoemaker looks right at me.

But if I get him out of my head, it would be like leaving my prison cell. You see, *I don't want to leave.* If I leave, it would be as though YOU win.

No, *you* would win.

Fuck that. I don't want to give you the satisfaction of curing me. People like you and my dad fucked me and now I want reparations. I want YOU to take care of me the rest of my life. FUCK YOU. I DON'T WANT TO GET BETTER. WHAT DO YOU THINK ABOUT THAT?

No response. I notice a serious expression on Dr. Shoemaker's face.

Lou, let's take a couple of days off. I'll be in touch with you.

Two days after that, I receive a letter addressed to me from Dr. Shoemaker. Inside the envelope is a one-page handwritten letter. This is exactly what it says.

April 22, 1983

Dear Mr. Panesi,

After much thought and consideration with regard to your therapy with me, I feel that we have reached an impasse. Please understand that now is the time to end our relationship. If you feel that you are in need of further therapy, please contact Robert J. Lanz, MD. Please do not contact my office for any further visits.

Sincerely,
Robert J. Shoemaker, MD

Unbelievable. The first thing I notice is his calling me "Mr. Panesi." He never called me that, *ever*. I was always Lou, or Luigi when he was kidding with me. I feel devastated. I've known Dr. Shoemaker since 1975. He's become the dad I never had. *All those years*—and now he's ending our relationship. I just can't believe it. I love Dr. Shoemaker.

And now I have to find a way to live without him.

CHAPTER 26
December 15, 1986: My Dream Fulfilled

"In the depth of winter, I finally learned that there was within me an invincible summer."

- Albert Camus

After I received Dr. Shoemaker's letter, I was shattered. It hit me that I could no longer rely on him to "save" me. I was going to have to take action on my own. I immediately contacted Dr. Lanz only to find that he wasn't much older than I was. This confused me. I was under the impression that any psychiatrist would be able to take care of me, but my first thought was that I didn't want *this* young guy to be the one. I had only a handful of visits with him when I realized he was no Dr. Shoemaker, so I stopped seeing him. Yet I knew I needed to see *someone*. I then began seeing Dr. Lester Bolanovich, who was Dr. Shoemaker's colleague. Because he was almost the same age as Dr. Shoemaker, that made me feel better.

Realizing no one could ever take Dr. Shoemaker's place, I felt my confidence grow. Maybe I'd come further than I thought during my last four years with Dr. Shoemaker.

Before long, I decided I needed to get back into flying. A wave of energy came over me. I knew I had to either sink or swim—no one would hold my hand anymore. I felt more determined than ever to get on with the airlines. I just knew I could do it.

So I went to the local airport and hired an instructor to help me get my flying skills to where they used to be. I wanted to become current with all of my ratings. This took a few weeks.

I wasn't positive if I could handle the problem I'd had with authority-figure men, but I was determined to see if all of the work with Dr. Shoemaker had paid off. There was only one way to find out—I had to reenter the work force. Most important, I had to do *something*. I didn't have Dr. Shoemaker to use as a crutch anymore.

So I sent out resumes to commuter airlines along the east coast. After only a few months, I received an offer to fly with a commuter airline out of Salisbury, Maryland. This was the break I needed. I packed up my things and moved to Salisbury, which was tough because it spelled the end for Bea and me. We both knew it would be hard to continue a long-distance relationship.

As I worked at this new job, I saw how far I had come. Although I still felt slightly uncomfortable dealing with men in authority, my distress was nothing like it used to be. In fact, I even made friends with a few of the captains I flew with. This was a big accomplishment.

There is no doubt in my mind that if Dr. Shoemaker had not ended our relationship when he did, I would have used him as a crutch for the rest of his life. I'm now sure that part of being a great therapist means knowing when to say goodbye. He did what he needed to do; he kicked me out of the nest. He realized this was the right time. I was scared to leave and he knew it. I'm also positive that if he had not ended our relationship, I would have gotten worse, not better.

I was only at my job in Salisbury for eight months when a better opportunity presented itself. A company out of Bridgeport, Connecticut, offered me a job to fly as captain on a twin-engine commuter plane all over New England. I flew into Martha's Vineyard and Nantucket and Boston and New York. I even met a girl named Marie and we became close. Even her mom and dad liked me. This was a big deal to me—I was making my way in the world.

Eventually, an even better job came open in Cincinnati and I took it. This was my last stepping-stone before getting on with a major airline. I had worked there two years when Piedmont Airlines called me and offered me a job on December 15, 1986! My dream would be fulfilled; I would be flying large jets all over the U.S. and maybe even the world.

As it turned out, it only took 3 years and 7 1/2 months after Dr. Shoemaker let me go for me to reach my dream. It never would have happened if he hadn't released me.

Since I started flying with Piedmont, I've flown into every major city in the U.S. I've also flown jumbo jets into Rome, Paris, and many other European cities. I've met many famous people on my flights. Right after I got hired, I met a woman on one of my flights named Elizabeth. We dated three years and got married in 1990. From North Carolina, she was a graduate of Texas Christian University in Fort Worth, Texas. We lived in Winston-Salem. I often told her about Dr. Shoemaker and how he'd helped me. She was highly supportive of me and learned a lot about what I'd gone through.

At the height of my career (before the terrorist events of September 11, 2001), I was making a salary of over $200,000 a year. More than the money, I really enjoyed the incredible respect I got. Doctors and lawyers would bring their kids up into the cockpit to meet me and look inside. Every time that happened, I'd recall when I worked as a janitor in a hotel and felt terrified to pick up my paycheck. That was only a few years before!

I've experienced an unbelievable life. I've lived at both the low end of the scale and the high end. I've seen how the transformation took place, both while I was seeing Dr. Shoemaker and afterward, too.

In the 20 years I've been with the airlines, I have pretty much kept my past to myself. I've told only a handful of pilots my story. And it's funny because each one of them said the same thing—that I should write a book. Someday I will . . .

EPILOGUE

"Gratitude is not only the greatest of virtues, but the parent of all others."

- Cicero

Dr. Shoemaker died on March 5, 1985; he was only 66 years old.

I heard the news after calling Dr. Bolanovich's secretary. I'd asked her how he was doing when I heard he'd entered the hospital. The secretary's exact reply was "I'm sorry, Louis, but Dr. Shoemaker passed away this morning."

When I heard the words "passed away," I dropped the phone, fell to the floor, and started wailing. Out of my mouth came a primal, blood-curdling scream. "NO, NO, NO."

I thought, "How could he be dead? How could *he* be dead and *me* still be alive? This isn't possible. How could he leave me?"

Even though I had not seen him in almost two years, I'd always known where he was. Every day, I could depend on his being in his Pittsburgh office at 121 University Place helping people. Suddenly, all I could think of was "I am alone now. He won't be there if I need him. I'm *really* all alone now."

I was in shock. I couldn't see straight. I felt as though all of the blood had drained from my head. "Can I make it on my own?" I asked. I had been making it on my own for years, but in that moment, it was all different. My heart was broken. The man who had single-handedly saved my life was gone.

I screamed, "Don't leave me, Dr. Shoemaker. Don't leave me. Please don't leave me." I wished *I* were dead instead of him.

I worried that I had killed him. "Did all of those years on the couch when I screamed at him every day contribute to his death?" I wondered. He did his job and let me vent my anger, but surely that process must have taken a toll on him.

Dr. Shoemaker was born on February 7, 1919, in Erie, Pennsylvania, and lived exactly 24,133 days. In his past he had served as president of the Pennsylvania Psychoanalytic Association. He was also the superintendent of Woodville Mental Hospital, one of the largest mental hospitals in Pennsylvania. Dr. Shoemaker was also on the faculty at the University of Pittsburgh School of Medicine.

He *had* to have been one of the greatest psychiatrists who'd ever lived. Are there any other mental health professionals on earth who could have done what he did for me? I don't think so.

When he met me, I was afraid of my own shadow. A lost soul. I couldn't look any human being in the eye and especially couldn't look at girls. I believed that all men were monsters. I didn't know how to shake hands. I was homeless, barely working as a janitor. Without Dr. Shoemaker, I would have bounced from one homeless shelter to the next until I likely would have been institutionalized. I don't think I would have lived very long.

At the beginning of my treatment, I remember being afraid of him, so in order to reach me, he first had to break down many barriers. He used a lot of stories to get me to listen to him and make me laugh. He told me a lot about fishing and hunting and sex. He really made me laugh when he talked about sex and let me know he "looked" at young women. Wow, that was *big*. After talking to me about sex, I would leave his office thinking, "Why am I so afraid of this guy? He's pretty much a pervert." When I told him as much, he would laugh and say, yes, he was a pervert. Hearing that was a huge moment in my relationship with him.

All of those stories he told me served a purpose. It made me "look" at him as he talked. For me, it was incredibly difficult to look at a grown man who was actually looking at *me!*

These talks helped me come out of my shell and not put him on a pedestal. He pulled out all of the stops to get to me. This is where Dr. Shoemaker shined. His methods may have been controversial and unorthodox, but he did what he had to do.

He was also careful to be gentle with me. I was like a little squirrel and he knew a quick movement of any kind would have frightened me.

I'll never forget one session near the beginning of my treatment with him. He did something that proved to be pure brilliance. I was talking intently about something. I don't recall exactly, but most likely it was about my dad or my grandfather. I was sitting in my chair in front of his desk looking right at him. *And he acted totally uninterested in me!* He even looked down and doodled on a piece of paper. This went on for about five minutes until I finally blurted out, **"What the fuck are you doing? I'm talking to you and you aren't even listening to me."**

Here's what he did. Like a little boy, he put down his pen, folded his hands together on his desk, and acted like I was *his* boss. This hit a nerve in me and I started crying really hard. Still with my head down, I yelled, "How could you let me talk to you like that? Here you are, seeing me for nothing and I'm yelling at you. You should have said, 'Who do you think you are, you little piece of shit? Here I am seeing your ass for nothing and you've got the balls to talk to me like that? FUCK YOU, you loser.'" Instead, he replied, "That's what your dad would have said, isn't it?" Still crying hard with my head down, I managed to nod yes. He then said to me in a soft, gentle voice, "I'm not your dad, Lou." Those words made me cry even harder.

I now know that he did this intentionally. He set me up to blast him— like throwing a fastball right down the middle of the plate for me to hit. And I did. He wanted me to stand up to an authority figure. He wanted me to let him have it. He knew that I had never done that before, ever. That incident was so painful for me, but to be able to yell at a grown man and have him respect my position was an important step toward my becoming more mature.

What a man. I didn't know it at the time, but I was witnessing a master at work.

Dr. Shoemaker was not stuck on himself. He knew he was a great doctor, but by the same token, he was willing to say, "It's all bullshit." That was the first piece of wisdom he gave me. I have never forgotten that. Here he was, possibly the greatest therapist who ever lived, telling me that all of those books on his bookshelves were bullshit. In one way, they are. It all comes down to being a man. Being real. He was a cool guy who never hid behind his title of M.D.

Still, I believe to this day that I contributed to his early death, even slightly. He took a lot of abuse from me during my four years on the couch. In this book, I cover only part of the experience, but the total picture would span a thousand pages. It was like the movie *The Exorcist* in which the priest had to take a lot of verbal abuse from the demon in order to save the little girl's life. And in the movie, the priest dies.

I want to mention that some mental health professionals have contacted me about the way Dr. Shoemaker let me go. They told me they felt that he released me prematurely, even calling it "unprofessional." One psychoanalyst used the words "acted out" in reference to his actions. Of course, this was hard for me to hear. I always wanted to put Dr. Shoemaker on a pedestal.

Today, I acknowledge that it may be possible that he ended our relationship a little soon. I have dealt with that and I am fine with it. Dr. Shoemaker helped make me a tough man. I can deal with a lot. He taught me to go with my gut instincts. Yes, it's possible that he was not "perfect," but he was close. I think his results speak for themselves.

As I write this, I am a 54-year-old middle-aged man. I am only two years younger than Dr. Shoemaker was when I first met him. It's funny because he seemed so old to me back then. In reality, he was still a young man.

What has happened over the years? Where am I today?

While I was flying for the airlines, I was able to travel the world. I had an exciting job. Yet deep down, something wasn't quite right with me, so I went to a doctor. I soon learned that I suffered from post traumatic stress disorder (PTSD). After I was diagnosed with PTSD, the doctor put me on an antidepressant. It helped me, but also disqualified me from flying because pilots aren't allowed to take any medication. Right now, I'm on medical leave from US Airways.

My marriage to Elizabeth ended in 1994 after four years. We still remain friends.

Frank Palombi, the boy in Chapter 5, is now a captain with United Airlines. He still lives near Carnegie, Pennsylvania, and we keep in touch.

Reba and Harold Siebert, both 94, still live in the same house in Carnegie.

My mom died in 2006.

Dr. Gibson, 92, lives in a nursing home. Without Dr. Gibson, I would have been doomed. My destiny changed when he handed me that piece of paper with Dr. Shoemaker's information. TV's Dr. Phil would call that my life's "defining moment."

I still bite my fingernails and have scars on my back, but I don't worry about them anymore. Instead, I look at them as symbols of where I came from. And it's OK.

I am a very lucky man. In my life, I have crossed paths with these great men: Dr. Gibson, Dr. Shoemaker, and Roberto Clemente. I was fortunate to have watched Roberto Clemente play at Forbes Field. In my opinion, he is, to this day, the greatest baseball player that I have ever seen. His talent is impossible to describe; you'd have to have seen him in action to believe it.

The same could be said about Robert Shoemaker. I have spoken to Dr. Shoemaker's son about this book. From him, I learned that his father never mentioned me when he was at home. I also learned that Dr. Shoemaker never told his colleague, Dr. Bolanovich, about giving me eight years of therapy for free. So I'm the only living person who knows exactly what Dr. Shoemaker did for me. And now, it's up to *me* to do my best and tell the world about *him*.

Every time I hear Simon and Garfunkel's song "Bridge Over Troubled Water" I think that Dr. Shoemaker is talking to me. It's like he wrote the words for me.

> *When you're weary, feeling small*
> *When tears are in your eyes I will dry them all*
> *I'll take your part when darkness comes*
> *Your time has come to shine,*
> *All your dreams are on their way.*

I want to thank Dr. Shoemaker and all of the therapists who have worked with me over the years. It's taken me 54 years but I am finally happy. Today, I feel confident and I like myself.

I have a lot to live for.

Lou Panesi
September, 2009

***

"It is the responsibility of every adult . . . to make sure that children
hear what we have learned from the lessons of life and
to hear over and over that we love them
and that they are not alone."

\- Margaret Wright Edelman

***

.

AFTERWORD

**Comments from People Who
Have Lived Lou's Journey with Him**

MARCA STOREY
Therapist that worked with Lou

Writing this tribute to Dr. Shoemaker is the best thing Lou can do to honor the memory of Dr. Shoemaker, the man who became his source of love and healing. Dr. Shoemaker *did* save Lou's life; I believe this to be true. He was a master in his field, which is what Lou needed.

Lou clearly benefited from their years of intense psychotherapy, especially when compared with what managed care currently offers—brief, solution-focused therapy in which clients are expected to be healed in 20 sessions or less. This type of therapy would not have been successful for Lou.

The verbal, psychological, and physical abuse in Lou's life was massive. Thank goodness Dr. Shoemaker saw the jewel and potential in Lou. He has shared many painful sessions with me regarding the traumas of his childhood and the self-esteem issues he struggles to overcome today. The memories of past abuses have had a stranglehold on him. Writing this book is cathartic—very meaningful and necessary. It has afforded him the opportunity to complete the last phase of his healing.

Lou is compassionate, kind, personable, and sensitive to others' feelings. His biggest hurdle now is interpersonal relationships—reaching out to others and receiving feedback that tells him he is worthy. Lou has chosen to live an authentic life. He realizes in his journey that he has to be honest with himself.

Lou also believes no one can tell his story like he can—especially given his photographic memory for details. This book truly comes from his heart and gives him a creative place to put his energy. Writing it has helped him develop confidence. He's no longer like a car running with the pedal constantly on the accelerator.
I believe Lou speaks the truth. He's courageous and not afraid to self-disclose about his life if he thinks it will help others. For many others who are wounded and hurting, this book may be a powerful roadmap for healing.

121 University Place is Lou's ultimate way to give back. That is how people heal!

ELIZABETH HOLMES
Lou's wife from 1990 to 1994

In my opinion, Lou was extremely fortunate to find Dr. Shoemaker. He became the father figure Lou never had and so desperately needed. It is one thing in life to never have had a father and to try to overcome the psychological repercussions that occur as a result of those circumstances. However, it is another situation entirely to have a father who sets a bad example at every turn. That's what Lou had to endure. Then for Lou to be able to overcome the trauma to a great extent was amazing and something that Dr. Shoemaker can be credited with.

Dr. Shoemaker helped guide Lou during an important time in his life, which in turn helped form Lou's personality. This gave him the opportunity to formulate goals for himself, which gave him independence.

Dr. Shoemaker felt so much compassion for Lou and, in turn, never gave up on his being able to overcome the psychological damage that had occurred when he was growing up. Dr. Shoemaker did a phenomenal job in his treatment of Lou, giving Lou an opportunity for a normal life.

When I met Lou, he was a very intelligent, quick-witted man who was kindhearted, honest, and trustworthy. He inherited many of his traits from his paternal grandmother who loved him very much. Lou and I met in March 1987 when he was a 727 pilot. We were married on August 4, 1990, Lou's 35th birthday. Lou moved out around our first anniversary. The entire year we lived together, we never had an argument of any kind. As it turned out, Lou needed his space. He preferred living as a bachelor. I knew a lot about Lou when I married him; as it turned out, I didn't know everything.

Lou knew that I would be hurt when he left; he just couldn't help the circumstances that led him to that decision. I realize now that Lou was trying to protect himself. I was aware that he had psychological scars from his childhood and thought I understood his trauma. I believed he had dealt with his issues; the truth is that he was processing things I wasn't privy to.

I hope it is therapeutic for him to write this book and I do wish him the best always.

CHUCK STEINMILLER
Childhood friend and "closer than a brother" today

I've known Lou since I was seven and Lou was four. We were neighbors in Carnegie, Pennsylvania.

I saw firsthand how Dr. Shoemaker was a father figure to Lou. I saw how Dr. Shoemaker helped him socialize with people and function in society to the point that he was able to become a successful pilot. He recognized what Lou needed most—a caring father/son relationship. And like a father, the doctor recognized he had to let Lou go at some time.

When Dr. Shoemaker told Lou "you write your story," he knew that would be part of Lou's therapy. It would mean looking on his early life and dealing with it.

From my perspective, because of Lou's work with Dr. Shoemaker, I gained a lifelong friendship. I'm one of a few people Lou has a trusting relationship with. Even today, we talk every day and we can talk about anything. I'd say we're closer than most brothers. That's much different than when he was a teenager working at the hotel and felt too scared to get his paycheck from his supervisor. It's much different today than in the mid-70s when Lou was so shut down, he couldn't remember being an usher at my wedding or playing the drums at the reception.

His work with Dr. Shoemaker made our lifelong friendship possible.

REBA SIEBERT
Long-time neighbor who provided a safe haven
for Lou in Carnegie, Pennsylvania

Lou had a miserable childhood. His dad and grandfather wouldn't let him have or do anything. Even when he was seven months old and crying, his dad put Lou and his mom on the street in the winter at two in the morning. They came seven houses down the block to our place and stayed here until they were able to move to California.

After Lou came back to live with his dad permanently at age ten, he still had to sneak down the back alley to come to see us. He told me then he wanted to write a book about all the horrible things in his life. I'm happy he's done it.

I did whatever I could for him all his life. He's a very thoughtful man. He even sent my husband flowers and a beautiful card for his 91st birthday.

PHOTOS

Photos from Lou's Life

1956 with Grandparents

Grandma 1 year old

with Dad 5 months old

4th Grade in California

Grandma and Grandpap

JAN   56

Grandma

Reba and Harold Siebert

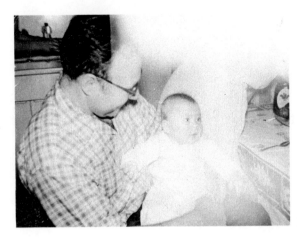

Dad 5 months old

8 months old

with Mom 2nd Birthday

August 1962 with Grandparents

Grandparents and Dad 1969

Summer 1977 Cincinnati, Ohio

H.S. Graduation, June 1973

College Grad 1978

Bea 8-4-83

leaving Rome

Marie Hickman 1984

8-4-90 Liz

Roberto Clemente

Dr. William S. Gibson, Dermatologist

with fitness expert Denise Austin 1988

12-15-86 New Hire Photo

US Airways 1989

current photo of author

Jill Eilenberger
Charlotte, NC Therapist that greatly influenced my life

Ohio University

Frank Palombi 1972

Frank Palombi 1972

Frank Palombi
United Airlines Captain
(*My friend from chapter 5*)

Rendering of Dr. Shoemaker's Office

121 University Place

121 University Place

God bless you Dr. Shoemaker

LaVergne, TN USA
03 February 2011
214962LV00004B/225/P